The

Cubicle

Survival Guide

The
Cubicle
Survival Guide

*Keeping Your Cool
in the Least Hospitable
Environment on Earth*

JAMES F. THOMPSON

VILLARD • NEW YORK

None of the characters depicted in the following pages are actual people. Like Shrek and Spiderman, you cannot call them, date them, or ask them to join your class action lawsuit. The characters found in this book are a combination of the author's experiences, observations, and imagination. Any similarities between the characters in this book and real people can be attributed to the shared inhumanity of cubicle life.

A Villard Books Trade Paperback Original

Published in the United States by Villard Books, an imprint of The Random House Publishing Group, a division of Random House, Inc., New York.

VILLARD and "V" CIRCLED design are registered trademarks of Random House, Inc.

ISBN 978-0-8129-7676-2

Library of Congress Cataloging-in-Publication Data

Thompson, James F.
The cubicle survival guide: keeping your cool in the least hospitable environment on earth / James F. Thompson.
p. cm.
ISBN 978-0-8129-7676-2 (alk. paper)
1. Work—Social aspects—Humor. 2. Microcomputer workstations—Humor. 3. Office politics—Miscellanea—Humor. 4. Work environment—Humor.
HD6955.T5 2007
650'.102/07—dc22
2006050164

Printed in the United States of America

www.villard.com

2 4 6 8 9 7 5 3 1

For Mom and Dad,
who taught me how funny being serious is

CONTENTS

INTRODUCTION

Welcome to the Cube!

Cubicles. We all know people who work in them. They are our aunts, sons, best friends, former lovers, and current neighbors. Besides five-foot fabric walls, cubicle dwellers share an important commonality: Someone they work with thinks they are totally wacko. And they're right! Your aunt Debbie picks her nose in her cubicle. Twenty-four-year-old Larry Combs cries in his. Margaret Dunn gossips with her best friend about hooking up with her ex-husband in the parking garage. The religious man who runs Neighborhood Watch steals bagels from the kitchen and hoards them in his desk. Cubicles have a significant influence on human behavior, both professionally and personally. From how we decorate cubes to the way we socialize in them, cubicles play a major role in the manner in which we, and others, define ourselves.

Why Cubicle *Dwellers?*

Families live in houses. Animals inhabit ecosystems. Celebrities reside on estates. Troops occupy positions. Gollums (Precious!) cower in fear. Aliens exist on planets. Employees dwell in cubicles. So why don't people inhabit or occupy cubicles? Surely employees exist in cubicles. Some undoubtedly cower. Others, especially workaholics, live in their cubicles more than they do their homes or apartments. Yet the commonly accepted terminology when describing the relationship between employees and their cubicles is *dwell*. Don't delude yourself. It is a derogatory word. One better left to characterize mammals hibernating in the winter than human beings making an honest living. There is, and always has been, a negative connotation to the word. "Come on. Forget about getting drunk at the office happy hour and hooking up with that cretin sales representative. You're making yourself crazy. Don't *dwell* on it." Nevertheless, people who work in cubicles are referred to as *cubicle dwellers;* and, like other abominations of our cultural lexicon such as *white-collar criminals* (they're regular criminals, just like the people who steal your car or silver), *fanny pack* (it goes around your waist, and the word *fanny* is just ridiculous), and *whatever* (have the stones to say *I don't care* like they did in the old days), it appears the phrase *cubicle dweller* is here to stay. Ignoring that the expression is popular and commonly used would undermine the purpose of a survival guide, so despite its ugly form and implicit meaning, *cubicle dweller* is used throughout the following pages whenever necessary. When possible, other more respectful and resonant words such as *inhabitant, resident,* and *occupier* are used as civilized alternatives. Perhaps one day the noble *cubicle resident* will emerge from the dark shadow contemporary society insists on casting over what has become our nation's new middle class.

Cubicle *Farm*? Really?

It's time to set the record straight. *Cubicle farm* is misleading. Employees are not laying eggs, being milked (at least not literally), or getting slaughtered for their hind parts or loins. Real farms in America are being foreclosed or turned into massive breeding compounds for animals that have more steroids in them than the 1988 Russian Olympic women's gymnastics team. For some reason we have decided, as if it were a nine-hundred-pound cow impervious to all modern diseases, to butcher the word *farm* beyond recognition. We *farm* out work to others, we institutionalize crazy cousins at the *funny farm*, we make people sit at desks, choked by neckties and leg stockings, and hide them from the sun and wind in the *cubicle farm*. None of these actions or environments, of course, even remotely resembles what is commonly considered a farm. It doesn't make sense. Certainly somewhere along the way the term *farm* was molested by a person or persons of significant influence, for reasons unknown to the public.

Humanity is broken down into ethnicity, religious affiliations, countries, regions, states, provinces, prefectures, cities, towns, counties, villages, and areas. There is no reason why people organized into smaller sections and groupings cannot take advantage of existing nomenclature such as *communities, neighborhoods, streets,* and *blocks.* Even though people are more than happy to complain about the US Postal Service, these demarcations of location work well, and have worked so for a long time. On top of that, these terms indicate civilized and cultivated collections of human beings, and so it is only appropriate that they be applied, at the very least metaphorically, to people who work in locations just as organized as the locations where they live.

The phrase *cubicle farm* is used sparingly throughout this book. More humane and less bovine phrases such as *cubicle com-*

munity, cubicle neighborhood, cubicle block, and *cubicle street* are used in its place.

CUBE>QUEST

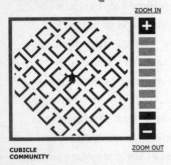

ZOOM IN

ZOOM OUT

**CUBICLE
COMMUNITY**

CUBICLE COMMUNITY: The *cubicle community* refers to the collective population of cubicle residents everywhere. The phrase acknowledges that people who work in cubicles are part of a distinct experience and environment. They all understand the impersonal nature of corporate life, the funny and disheartening aspects of working in the confinement of cubicles, and what it's like to work with others you have nothing in common with except a company. The cubicle community is a complex entity, more like an ecosystem or culture that has levels of complicated relationships, values, and governing forces. The cubicle community is like other communities commonly referred to, such as the bird-watching community, the gambling community, the gay community, and the car-enthusiasts community. The cubicle community is both local and international. It is perhaps the most often shared secular commonality among human beings other than universal experiences and innate emotions.

CUBE>QUEST

ZOOM IN

ZOOM OUT

**CUBICLE
NEIGHBORHOOD**

CUBICLE NEIGHBORHOOD: Much like the neighborhoods we all live in, the *cubicle neighborhood* is the area in which we work. The cubicle neighborhood can be designated according to several different criteria. For example, the cubicle community is often broken up into geographic sections such as the potted-plant cubicle neighborhood, the photocopier cubicle neighborhood, the motivational-poster cubicle neighborhood, and the near-the-window cubicle neighborhood. Other cubicle communities are broken down according to corporate structure even though they exist as one indistinguishable mass, including the accounting cubicle neighborhood, the programming cubicle neighborhood, and the marketing cubicle neighborhood.

CUBICLE BLOCK: The *cubicle block* usually consists of two to ten cubicles that share a cubicle street and often face one another. Cubicle blocks constitute cubicle neighborhoods the same as they do in areas where we live. And similar to the blocks you live on, you get to know those employees who work on the same cubicle block very well simply based on proximity. It is imperative to get along with the coworkers on your cubicle block. They know everything about you. They listen to your phone calls. They know if you are lazy or professional. They smell what you eat for lunch. They see what time you arrive at and leave from work. They ask about your significant others, family, loves, and hobbies. Just like the block you live on, cubicle blocks are where people learn to trust one another, complain to and about one another, help one another, and gossip about one another. Most likely, if you get promoted or fired, the people on your cubicle block will have a say in it. Think about it.

CUBE>QUEST

ZOOM IN

CUBICLE BLOCK

ZOOM OUT

CUBICLE STREET: Like the street you live on, your *cubicle street* is the avenue of transportation just outside your cubicle

CUBE>QUEST

ZOOM IN

+

ZOOM OUT

−

CUBICLE STREET

entrance. And like the street you live on, do not enter your cubicle street without first checking traffic both ways. Your colleagues could be quietly but hastily about to pass your work space with a steaming cup of coffee in their hands. A little precaution goes a long way on the cubicle street. Unfortunately, unlike the street you live on, cubicle streets generally do not have names, traffic lights, or rules of interaction. So be careful. Also, be conscientious of any decoration you put on the outside wall of your cubicle. Those passing by will, of course, see it, and any attempt to advertise your political beliefs or religious values may not be appreciated in the corporate setting. Save the STERN FOR GOVERNOR poster and the nativity scene for your front lawn.

How to Use This Book

This book is designed to empower cubicle inhabitants with information regarding hardships and potential career-ending problems encountered while at work. The chapters address important issues that are common, if not daily, occurrences at the office. Unlike other treatments of cubicle life in print, on television, and in the movies, this book does not intend to simply make fun of the cubicle community and mock managers, quirky colleagues, and the impersonal omnipotence of the corporate paradigm. This book goes the extra mile by actually serving as a functional survival guide that employees can consult should they need advice, a laugh, or something more inexplicably surreal than managers, quirky colleagues, and the impersonal corporate paradigm that has replaced their child-hood dreams. Yet have faith. This book will demonstrate that cubicle life is not as bad as you think it is. Cubicle life is, how-ever, just as funny as you think it is.

The
Cubicle
Survival Guide

CHAPTER ONE

Perspective

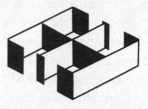

Over the centuries humankind has adapted to all kinds of environments and climates. As our surroundings evolve, so do we. Eskimos adjusted to arctic conditions by building igloos and hunting in sealskin canoes. In Los Angeles, where the weather is perfect, people have decided they need to be perfect, too, and survive on green-tea hand lotion and Botox injections. For thirteen hundred years the residents of Inuyama, Japan, have provided for their families with *ukai*, a traditional style of river fishing that utilizes cormorants on leashes. Nevertheless, despite its impressive history, the human race has had difficulty harmonizing with the proliferation of cubicle environments. Some treat their cube like an Exxon bathroom; others, like a fabric chamber of corporate policy. Perhaps in the future the harsh cubicle landscape won't produce a homogenized corporate humankind, but an individualistic Australian-like wildlife of humanity, teeming with evolutionary freaks such as the platypus, koala bear, and saltwater crocodile. Yet to envision the future of cubicles, we must take a look at their history.

Where did cubicles officially come from? And why?

Cubicles were originally designed so that office workers could freely discuss and trade ideas without being tempted to shake hands or exchange pictures of their children. Every dimension of the cubicle partition has a specific, tactical purpose. Though invented back in the 1960s by Bob Probst, a professor of fine arts at the University of Colorado, cubicles became an unpopular cultural phenomenon in America around the same time actual money was replaced by the idea of stock options and entry-level twenty-somethings began renting limousines for no reason other than it was a Saturday night.

Today those twenty-somethings drive SUVs, and the only fallout from the fusion-like implosion of the dot-com era is a nuclear winter of cubicle farms inhabited by lithe humans who toil in confined spaces in exchange for compensation. Despite sensitivity training, ergonomic keyboards, and much-needed health insurance that includes psychotherapy, cubicle dwellers can't escape the oppressive monotony and homogenization of their existences. Fear not, *The Cubicle Survival Guide* is here to help.

Shhhh . . . They're Not Real Walls

First, know your surroundings. Most cubicle dwellers have no idea what their walls are made of or why. Today most cubicles are relatively uniform and constructed from a one- or two-inch steel frame that supports a wood core wrapped in neutrally colored fabric so it can be utilized as a bulletin board. Many cubicles come with various accessory options such as shelves, cabinets, or over-desk storage. However, the characteristic that has made the cubicle omnipresent in capitalistic ventures across the planet is that it is, as one seller puts it, "Easy to assemble and move without tools." In other words, you can reconfigure how and where employees work within minutes.

So don't get comfortable. The days of lifelong employment and company loyalty are long gone. Global and national economies are constantly ebbing and flowing, sometimes drastically, which means businesses are, too. They need the ability to adapt and reconfigure their mission statements, their corporate profiles, and, yes, their employee structure. Likewise, employees are often, even in their own cubicles, searching for the next step in their professional lives.

Cubicles serve as the drab metaphor and stark, impersonal reality of the modern employee–employer relationship: Expendability rules. This is why one can earn an advanced degree in human resources.

Considering America's long love affair with the right to privacy and individuality, it seems paradoxical that forty million of us voluntarily work in cubicles. The traditional American pioneer spirit seems at odds with the reality of our modern culture. So what happened to our American love of distinctiveness? Technology. The cubicle farm, after all, was cultivated around the bumper crop of computer technology. However, before you blame Bill Gates and Steve Jobs for your carpal tunnel and slipped vertebrae, remember that cowboys today use high-tech cell phones to herd cattle and the real

CUBE TIP

Never gossip in your cubicle, particularly about human resource people. They specialize in filling jobs, including the one you have and perhaps the one you want. Office gossip often begins with someone forgetting that a cubicle wall is not a real wall.

James Bond chases enemies of the state across software and bandwidths. So don't despair. You're not the only one interacting with the rest of the world through your computer screen. And you're certainly not the only one who feels depersonalized by the superconnected world we live in. Cubicles are the result of our times, not our personalities.

The Standard Office Workstation
Also Known as a Cubicle

WORKSTATION INVENTORY

1. Seafoam-green ergonomic company-issued chair (x 1)
2. Floor file cabinets (x 2)
3. Panel-mounted storage units (x 2)
4. Multi-line phone with conference feature (x 1)
5. Slate-gray fabric privacy panel: large (x 4)
6. Slate-gray fabric privacy panel: half-size (x 2)
7. Refurbished 2002 desktop PC (x 1)
8. Form MS001: Mission Statement (x 1)

Corporations often have difficulty appreciating individual talents because they focus on the bottom line: how the department is performing as a whole. Most American cubicle dwellers know that business is about profit margins, and they accept this reality. Unfortunately, the folks who communicate with "corporate" often only notice individual office workers when they're doing something wrong. Like eating microwave popcorn and stinking up the hallway. Or inappropriately expressing themselves with sexy calendars, deeply personal screensavers, and outlandish attempts to make their work spaces quaint and comfortable. For some reason even the most intelligent, educated, and well-meaning people cross the invisible corporate line.

For example, no one at Cubers International knows that Larry worked fifty-five hours last week. Everyone knows, however, thanks to the picture tacked onto his cubicle wall, that he got trashed last Halloween.

Kathy over in Cubers International's executive resources loves going to the beach in a bikini; apparently she got a boob job sometime between the summer of 2004 and 2005.

According to the buttons pinned along the top of her cubicle wall, Gertrude Patterson is ultraliberal and collected several souvenirs at the pro-rights rally last month. Her boss, a quiet neoconservative whose sparse office is decorated with a stuffed largemouth bass, not only silently disapproves of her buttons but is also allergic to the Ecuadorian tiger lily on her desk. He mentions his allergy problem to Carlton Frye in human resources, whom no one knows is not even registered to vote. Though Gertrude will never be fired because no one wants lawyers around, she will also never get a promotion. Decorating her cubicle with touchy political beliefs is in poor taste, and her inability to understand corporate decorum demonstrates a lack of perspective and emotional intelligence. Subconsciously the colleagues she has made uncomfortable will avoid interacting with her. Eventually, upset by her working conditions,

Gertrude will quit Cubers International. Unbeknownst to her, she'll quit her next job for the same reasons. And the next. Two years later she'll move back in with her mother and begin collecting stray cats.

When the police come to arrest Gertrude Patterson because of neighborhood health code violations, they will find 738 cats, many of them covered in fleas and living in the bedroom walls. When they escort Gertrude into the backseat of the police car, she will sob to an officer, "Life is not fair." She's right. It's not. Especially life in a cubicle. It needs a guidebook. Today Gertrude would be running her own Fortune 500 telecommunications company if only she'd had a copy of *The Cubicle Survival Guide*. Don't laugh. There is more to your job than how well you work. There's how well you "work."

Offices are like casinos in that they are designed around manipulating, controlling, and profiting from human behavior. Make no mistake, where you sit, the direction you face, the size and dimensions of your workstation were meticulously planned by people you have probably never met. So, welcome: Corporate America has been waiting for you.

Being stuck in a cubicle is like being stuck in an elevator. You have to assess the situation, assess the people you are with, and appreciate the circumstances. You may not like the state of affairs, but given the reality you must learn to not only like but also trust, the people you are with. Realize that your lives could go up, down, or nowhere . . . together.

The saying goes that democracy is the worst form of government, except for all the rest. Well, cubicle farms are the least desirable forms of working environments, except for all the rest. It's true. That is why so many of us agree to work in them. But keep it together. Our fantasies are just that. Fly-fishing guides complain about mosquitoes and idiot wealthy fishermen who catch their own earlobes. Supermodels throw up Greek salads and live off of cocaine and cigarettes for the sake of job security. Fame and wealth turned Tom Cruise into a paradoxical billionaire/homeless-acting man who believes in a religion that has nothing to do with the Middle East. Weirdo. Most world leaders have middle-management haircuts at best. Every member of Congress looks like he or she would steal NutraSweet packets from the coffee machine bin; given the option, they'd all steal packets of Equal because of its politically correct name. So when it comes down to working in a cubicle, you are dealing with regular folks: people who understand that the world is full of tough jobs, and that working at a cubicle is not a bad way to make a living.

These same sensible folks also realize it is their responsibility to protect themselves by being team players, socially savvy, and able to walk that fine line between being helpful and respectful of others without acting obsequious, wimpy, or contorting like a defenseless ant burning under the magnifying glass of corporate exploitation. The cubicle community, after all, is about fitting as many people as possible into a limited space. Cubicles are a unique means of arranging human beings and their behaviors. Navigating both the visible and invisible walls of the corporate landscape requires diligence.

This is where personality, education, upbringing, and your mothers and fathers come into play. Mind your manners. Remember *I'm okay, you're okay*. Hold the elevator door open for people making their way to it. Those forty-five seconds of your life could make a life-altering impression on some folks who don't know you, but may remember your gesture when you interview for that promotion next year. If they don't thank you for holding the door open, ignore them; they don't appreciate the little things that people do for free and probably won't appreciate the little things people do when they are getting paid. If cubicle inhabitants do not make defending their integrity and maintaining their self-respect a priority, then they run the very real risk of burnout, a common affliction in many jobs, particularly those surrounded by three fabric walls. Be able to give colleagues what they want without indulging their self-inflating efforts to bloat their egos by making you feel inferior. In essence, to survive or perhaps even thrive in the cubicle community you must have refined coping skills. You are, after all, part of the great monolithic machine known as the corporation.

The cubicle environment begins when you enter the building. Never forget this. Unfortunately, America today is seeing regular cubicle dwellers lose their rights. As long as you do your job well, corporate should never have rights to your blood, mental health history, home computer, religious beliefs, DNA, thoughts, political affiliations, urine, sexual orientation, subconscious, or secrets. If it does, then jobs in the cubicle community are no longer jobs, they are Hitleresque experiments on people who don't have the means or wealth to act like megalomaniacs who want to control human nature for the corporate bottom line, which they invariably explain away as health insurance expenses. Don't fall for it. If corporate only tested for infidelity, embezzlement, and greed, it would drop institutionalized behaviorism like a prostitute with a penis at a Las Vegas convention. But since that won't happen, remember this rule of thumb: How you decorate, organize, and behave in your cubicle is as important as how you dress, socialize, and perform your job.

Quick Quiz Self-Assessment

(1) True or False? Cubicles were invented during the Cold War in the basement of the Landsdown office building in Detroit, Michigan, by Dr. Brandon Flumdinger. He originally designed the partitions for the US military, which used the lightweight walls to construct fake headquarters, bunkers, and latrines in order to fool Soviet spy satellites.

(2) Complete the following the sentence: Having more than nine cats as pets is a sign that the owner . . .

    (a) can probably speak feline and see in the dark.

    (b) no longer has mice in the house.

    (c) was dehumanized by cubicle culture and now only relates to animals.

    (d) buys kitty litter in bulk.

(3) Identify the quote that is from an actual James Bond movie.

    (a) My name is Bond, James Bond, in cubicle L-17.

    (b) Moneypenny, the watercooler is empty.

    (c) If you get in trouble, James, push this button. It turns your stapler into a welding device.

    (d) None of the above.

ANSWERS:

(1) False. The cubicle was invented in the 1960s by Bob Propst, a professor of fine arts at the University of Colorado, so employees could freely exchange ideas and inspiration. (2) c. (3) d.

CHAPTER TWO

Decoration

Decorating your cubicle is complicated because it shows your bosses and colleagues who you are, both personally and professionally. Corporate America insists on neckties and business skirts, but real people are funnier, crazier, and less well adjusted than their work clothing suggests. Dan Summers in Cubers International's accounts payable department wears a custom-made Italian suit, makes seventy-two thousand dollars a year, and has a piece of driftwood wrapped in old fishing line in his cubicle. When perplexed visitors ask him about it, he simply answers, "I found that at the beach last summer. Isn't it awesome?"

Good business is about good relationships, so try not to confuse people who visit your cubicle. And try not to scare them, either. Mrs. Jenkins is a quiet mother of two who wears thick glasses and has pictures of dissected frogs and pigs tacked to her cubicle walls. She hasn't told anyone that to help her daughter with biology homework, she needs to understand circulatory and respiratory systems. Outside the office her colleagues call her "Mrs. Dahmer"; she always eats lunch alone.

Often, balancing your personality and freedom of speech with office politics and corporate sensibility is a difficult task.

Uninhibited decorating can be interpreted as a lack of professionalism or as a garish attempt to distance yourself from your surrounding environment. In contrast, surrendering self-expression to the bland landscape of bureaucracy can be seen as a lack of commitment, interest, or even individuality. So how do you know when too much is too much and too little is too little?

Begin by looking around you. Though corporate culture is a universal brand of working environment, each company and business is run and populated by individuals who create a collective, yet unique, atmosphere. Examine the cubicles in your environment to ascertain the general guidelines of decorum. More than likely you were never informed of these guidelines during orientation. In fact, such guidelines, though crucial, are rarely written down or addressed; they are an assumed set of rules, which makes them prime targets for manipulation, misinterpretation, or miscommunication. Some companies and CEOs encourage employees to express themselves. Others do not.

So look around. If you can't guess the religious or political affiliation of the people you work with, leave the DON'T BLAME ME, I VOTED FOR KERRY mug at home with your spiritually oriented candles. In America's diverse and litigious workforce, it is easy to offend someone willing to be a victim.

Like it or not, much of our lives are spent in cubes. Treat it like a home away from home, but a home with a powerful landlord and nosy neighbors. When you decorate your cubicle, be prepared to talk about each and every item.

Cubicle Classics

POSTCARDS: Postcards are an efficient means of letting your bosses and colleagues know that your life extends beyond your job. No matter how much you love your work, a postcard indicates that you appreciate palm trees, beaches, ancient architecture, exotic cultures, and places on earth that are not your cubicle. The American dream has many manifestations, but the most widespread version concerns people doing what

they love for a living. Reality in America, however, is different. Many of us—yes, even that incessantly perky twenty-nine-year-old former cheerleader with the handsome husband and convertible BMW—do not like our jobs. Subtly expressing the

sentiment *I'd rather be in a Corona commercial* is a manifestation of normalcy and even stoicism. People respect your perspective, because they live and work with the same feelings.

But don't go overboard with the postcard decorating option. For example, it's usually not a good idea to try to communicate humor via a postcard. Those people who slouch around shopping malls and patronize cacophonous shops that sell Magic 8-Balls, cardboard kaleidoscopes, and KISS posters may find a postcard of an obese woman on a moped funny, but your pregnant boss won't. A general rule to follow is that postcards should depict a special place and be sent from someone else to you. Any variations on this process are highly suspect.

Be prepared to discuss your postcards. Many cubicle dwellers tack onto their cushioned walls postcards they receive from friends and relatives; others tack up postcards they bought themselves for any number of reasons. If your uncle Jeff or cousin Veronda sent you a postcard from Istanbul or the coast of Maine, be prepared to discuss the Middle East, lobster rolls, and of course your family. In return your bosses and colleagues will happily reciprocate. If you tack up self-purchased postcards of the Sistine Chapel ceiling, Einstein's face, four kittens in a hat, or a monster truck, be prepared to talk about why that particular image appeals to you. At the very least, try to balance out your self-purchased postcard collection with real postcards sent to you by real people. That way colleagues will know you have friends in addition to likes and hobbies. Postcards are a great cubicle decoration choice. Each and every amiable conversation builds friendships and job security.

CUBE TIP

Bring your colleagues postcards or small trinkets from your travels that they can use to spice up their cubicles. This way they know you have been thinking of them, which helps build relationships, camaraderie, and business connections for the future.

FAMILY PHOTOS: In the soulless confines of a cubicle, pictures of family, friends, and pets instill warmth, love, and care. Especially pictures of children. On a Monday afternoon, when customers complain, management is tired from the weekend, and the building's temperature control is four months behind the weather, cubicle dwellers need to be reminded that they are working for someone other than themselves. Photos of spouses, significant others, and children put everything into perspective. Colleagues and bosses empathize with this condition; they are, after all, human, too.

This human connection brings co-workers closer together and helps build a sense of communal understanding and purpose. Remember that pictures of you and your friends on a drunken bender or photos of your gorgeous girlfriend posing in her tiny Dartmouth T-shirt are not as endearing to others as they are to you. Decorating your cubicle with pictures that are too personal will open your reputation to gossip and speculation. In an office setting, gossip, though at times unavoidable, is not how you want to be discussed. Be open with your colleagues, but keep control of what people know about you.

When leaving the confines of your cube and commenting on the pictures tacked up on fellow cube dwellers' walls, be careful what you say. In any discussions of family photos with colleagues it's important to listen carefully and be sincere, but cautiously so. In reality most of us are indeed ugly, warped, and possess faces that age like fallen apples on a driveway. Not all children are cute. Use words that don't force you to lie but also aren't too brutally honest. All older people can be described as "sophisticated." Most middle-aged people are "hilarious" in some way or another. Younger people are "sprite," and children are, of course, "adorable." Only use words such as *handsome, interesting,* and *beautiful* if you really believe that the person is handsome, interesting, or beautiful. Your colleagues do not appreciate being lied to. You probably don't, either.

FAMOUS PEOPLE: We all have our favorite musicians, Hollywood stars, sports heroes, and artists. Do not underestimate how much your proactive association with a widely known persona affects how you are perceived at work. A picture of a millionaire sex symbol such as Denzel Washington or Angelina Jolie does not make a cubicle dweller seem hip, fashionable, or cool. In fact, it makes a cubicle dweller seem immature, delusional, and desperate. Innocent infatuations are for the pubescent grade-schoolers who dream of actually getting phone calls and loving e-mails from pop icons. Mature men and women who work in cubicles will never receive a phone call or personal e-mail from a pop star, even if they have met the famous person and have a picture tacked above their monitor to prove it. For some reason this point is missed on many competent and successful cubicle dwellers. Even if you think Michael Jackson saved the human race with his "Thriller" dance, be aware that others might not appreciate your loyalty to his charisma and freakish charm. And never, ever moonwalk in an office building.

Furthermore, remember that every sports hero whom you endorse in your cubicle has a rival, who just may be your boss's hero. Just as with politics and religion, conversations about sports and competition can spiral into a counterproductive and even detrimental argument about conflicting values and geographic loyalties. Don't be paranoid, but be aware. When it comes to pictures of famous people, remember to be yourself; just keep in mind that stalkers and serial killers also tack pictures of people they've never met onto their walls.

SCREENSAVERS: Long gone are the days of twirling sticks of light, colorful bouncing orbs, and psychedelic patterns as screensavers. Now monitors the size of car windshields display football schedules superimposed over stadiums, the Egyptian pyramids under a pale moon, and three-dimensional digital seascapes complete with schooling fish and scuttling crustaceans. As with postcards, photographs, and famous people, your screensaver is the result of a conscious decision on your part—one that will reflect on your reputation. So the same rules apply: Be yourself without revealing anything too personal or antago-

nizing the corporate culture of your workplace. Supermodels stretched across sports cars, your infant niece breast-feeding at a family picnic, and your hysterical friends passed out on the lawn are all poor choices for screensavers. So are any images of handguns, shot glasses, and crucifixes.

Luckily, the Internet provides countless options for screensavers; cubicle dwellers everywhere should be able to find an image that suits their individual tastes and their company's aesthetic. Computer monitors are an essential and conspicuous staple in every cubicle, so be aware that the screensaver you decide on makes a statement. On a conscious and even subconscious level, you are trying to tell people something about you—*I love mountain ranges* or *My puppy catches Frisbees* or *I'm still wasted from last night and can't stop staring at the maze pattern.*

When in doubt, go with the black screen.

PLANTS: Small, low-maintenance plants add a welcome splash of life and color to any cubicle. However, turning your cubicle into the Babylonian Gardens makes you an obsessive freak just like the lady who collects anything "elephant" and the guy who buys old lunch boxes on eBay. As with your house, too much of anything is bad; unlike your house, going overboard with cubicle decorations is a professional matter, not a personal one. Keep the nurturing side of your personality in check. Not everyone shares your passion for flora. Show your team-player mentality by compromising your aesthetic sense with vapid corporate communalism: Strategically place a nice plant that doesn't smell, give people rashes, or eat flies in a safe place, where it won't get knocked over.

Remember that your plants are your responsibility. The people who vacuum the carpet around your chair and empty your trash will not water your plants for you. Like the corporation itself, they are concerned with the employees as a population, not as individuals. That is why drawing attention to yourself, especially unwanted attention, is not just a personal issue but ultimately a financial matter. If the plant dies in front of all your colleagues, it's your fault. You're not a murderer, but you are someone who can't take care of a plant.

VAGRANT SPACES: As in most neighborhoods, deadbeat dwellers in the cubicle farm can bring down the morale, beauty, and value of the surrounding environment. Instead of overgrown lawns and overflowing trash bins, unkempt cubicles become eyesores in already taxing environments filled with unnatural ventilation and lighting. The apathy that signifies their capitulation to corporate domination adds to the general depressing nature of office life. Disheveled cubicles serve as a hollow reminder that the corporation controls our salary, our upward mobility, our choice of clothing, our schedule, the light refracted by our retinas, and the air absorbed by our lungs. Some people give up. In a way, you can't blame them. Though most of us trudge on with smiles and our carefully placed plastic cup full of colorful pens and pencils, others have capitulated entirely. They stopped caring a long time ago, if they ever cared at all. Their cubicles speak for them. They have little, if anything tacked to their cushioned walls. Often you will notice faded newspaper clippings or a brochure of something that once meant something to them, before cubicle life crushed their dreams and made them fat.

Deadbeat cubicle dwellers for the most part are not bad people. They're simply dead inside. Sure, some will make attempts to decorate and demonstrate there is something left in there, but often these attempts merely highlight their demoralized souls. The "heart" made from spare tacks is a prime example of what Freud would call projection: The tack "heart" is hollow, misshapen, and made from sharp pieces of metal that hold things onto lifeless fabric walls. Another example is the "memo" motif. Tacking memos, office updates, and corporate policy briefings is a vain attempt to appear busy and engaged with one's responsibilities and surroundings. When asked about the content of their adornments, these cubicle dwellers commonly respond, "Huh?" They have no idea what the walls of the cubicles are saying. Especially about them.

People Who Work in Glass Cubicles

It is important not to judge too harshly the decorative tastes of others. We live in freedom, which means people can be as weird as they want as long as they are not hurting anyone or committing a crime. Some might argue, however, that freedom in the corporate world is different from freedom in the free world. They may argue, for example, that being told what clothes to wear is the exact opposite of freedom. Just because you decided to take the job doesn't mean you have all the power. In fact, accepting a job often means agreeing to giving away your time and freedom in exchange for money. It is a well-established compromise that capitalists, trust-fund kids, and polo players rely on for job security.

Without cubicle communities, wealthy families across the continent would have no need to differentiate themselves from regular people. They wouldn't need to wear pretentious slacks patterned with crossed golf clubs or tennis rackets, ties and shirts with embroidered sailboats, ladies' wide-brimmed hats with flower blossoms and lace streamers, and creepy old-lady brooches of oversize dragonflies or sea turtles. The family crest, finally, would be put to rest along with equally pompous attempts to glorify pedigree such as inbreeding and debutante balls. Thankfully most cubicle residents lack the financial resources to decorate their fabric walls with stuffed deer heads, medieval swords, or oil paintings from unpronounceable Italian provinces. In the cubicle community you're more likely to encounter Cuba Gooding Jr.'s face torn out of a tabloid

Cubicle Decoration

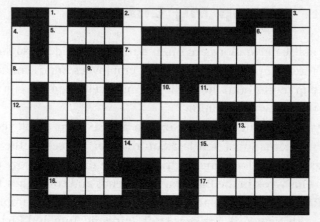

Across:

2. These add color to cubicles and infer their owners are caring and responsible.

5. If Lionel Ritchie worked in a cubicle, his soulful decorations would sing to his fellow employees, "_____, is it me you're looking for?"

7. Before decorating your cubicle, study the corporate culture and even your department's _____.

8. These types of photos should never be downloaded from your digital camera and offered for public viewing in your cubicle.

11. Pictures of these people in a cubicle indicate the employee is lonely and delusional.

12. Cubicle decorations can help exhibit an employee's _____.

14. Employees too cheap to purchase souvenirs from the beach decorate their cubicle desks with this.

16. Stuffed these should hang on the walls of your home, not your cubicle.

17. Pop culture obsessed employees tack this shiny type of movie star photo torn from magazines in their cubicles.

Down:

1. Photographs of these are great conversation openers and help build personal relationships with colleagues.

2. This demonstrates you have connections to a world beyond your fabric walls.

3. Nature-starved employees should never decorate their cubicle with these large scale plants.

4. These signify that during weekends and vacation time you go interesting places and are therefore a more interesting person than you reveal while at work.

6. Not every cubicle employee has the same sense of this.

9. How you decorate yourself with these is just as important as how you decorate your cubicle

10. A woman in this is a poor, and to some even an offensive, choice of screensaver.

11. Completely useless workplace information is often preceded with, "Oh, by the way, _ _ I..."

13. To show your are a part of the corporate family, an item featuring this image symbolizing the company is always a good addition to an employees decorative array.

15. Photos of you drunk at this type of party made famous in the movie Animal House should not be displayed in your cubicle.

magazine, fuzzy guinea pigs curled up in a sneaker, or a glossy calendar advertising the date and latest line of Rapala fishing lures.

Don't Pimp My Cubicle

Cubicle decorations are often a tribute to middle-class culture, but problems arise when employees impose middle-class pop mores onto the reality of midlevel corporate culture. Take the following situation.

Matt Lowe, lifelong Red Sox fan and six-year employee at Cubers International, left last Saturday for a week in the Bahamas with his longtime girlfriend. Little did Matt know that during his week in the Bahamas his friends and colleagues Tom and Richard would replace all of his cubicle Red Sox paraphernalia with New York Yankees stuff. Little did Tom and Richard know that during Matt's week in the Bahamas his girlfriend would dump him. Well, not exactly dump him, but get caught cheating on him with the hotel's tennis pro. Upon his return to work, Matt went ballistic. His Red Sox hat had been replaced with a New York Yankees hat. His laminated 2004 season schedule was replaced by a printout of the Yankees' upcoming schedule. Even the photograph of him and his dad at a Red Sox game in 1997 had been replaced with a photo of Johnny Damon in a Yankee uniform.

Matt never even had time to log on to his computer. After tossing his knapsack down his cubicle street, he launched into a tirade of expletives that in turn ignited a flurry of e-mails from the co-workers on his cubicle block. Within minutes everyone at Cubers International knew Matt was having a meltdown. Tom and Richard immediately came over to Matt's cubicle in an attempt to calm him down and beseech him to appreciate the humor in their redecorating. Matt countered their pleading with a litany of profanity followed by an extended discussion of how the Red Sox are the only thing anyone can trust in this world anymore. He raged about how "friends" like Tom and Richard could never understand a place like Boston. They could never understand how loyal the team and fans are to each other. They could never appreciate how someone like George Steinbrenner would never understand the true meaning of loyalty because he thinks he can just buy success with his billions and screw any tennis pro who happens to have a British accent. A brief yet interminably awkward moment of silence followed Matt's last comment. Taking one last glimpse of Johnny Damon in a New York Yankees uniform, Matt marched over to his knapsack, slung it over his shoulder, and disappeared into the elevator. He was never seen at Cubers International again. Though seven months later he was spotted on ESPN diving for a foul ball at Fenway Park.

The problem with having a sense of humor is that it is impossible to have one all the time. Never assume co-workers are having a good day before you actually interact with them and confirm their state of mind. Messing with someone's cubicle is rarely, if ever, funny. We have all been e-mailed pictures of cubicles filled with Styrofoam peanuts or crumpled newspapers, even cubicles wrapped in aluminum foil. Sure, these pictures are funny, but if something like that was actually done to *your* cubicle, you would probably be less than thrilled. In fact, you might even be angry. Of course you'd laugh, because that is what you are supposed to do, but deep down you'd be convinced such antics were a little sophomoric. (How do you retaliate? Roll the perpetrators' cubicles with toilet paper like you did in high school?) To make matters even worse, you might begin to visualize the time and effort behind the joke. Was so much work really worth a mere chuckle? Didn't these people have better things to do with their time? Why not let them go and give *you* the money they got paid to spread Styrofoam peanuts, ball up newspapers, and dispense aluminum foil? What if they did it because they don't like you? What if they're just pretending to joke around? Who has the audacity to go into other people's cubicles while they're gone—their private space!—and turn them upside down for a joke? Answer: Lots of people.

Never underestimate how much colleagues' cubicles mean to them. Many employees take great care to make sure their cubicles are comfortable. Some decorate with a meticulous Martha Stewart–like obsession, while others feel more at ease randomly filling their cubicles with trinkets, airport souvenirs, and cheeky bumper stickers. Harriet Graham "enlivens" her sage-colored fabric walls with complementary eggshell-white doily patterns (for use on holiday dessert trays) she bought at a CVS post-Christmas sale and matching eggshell-white push-pins. Her desk planner is also eggshell white, and just last week she bought a matching eggshell-white coffee mug with CRO-CHETERS NEVER UNRAVEL! written on it.

Kurt Hyman, on the other hand, has been using the same disposable paper coffee cup for thirteen days. It's his way of demonstrating his belief that our use-once-then-throw-away disposable society is senselessly ruining the environment. To further prove his point, Kurt has pictures of twenty-seven different types of endangered or extinct species tacked to his cubicle walls with slightly bent paper clips. "No need to buy thumbtacks with plastic grips that aren't biodegradable when you can just use a paper clip," he explains. "When you're done hanging stuff you can bend it back into a regular paper clip again. It's a recyclable resource." Though most of Kurt's colleagues are very understanding of his passion and the points he is attempting to make, some are not happy with the message tacked, by paper clips, to the outside of his cubicle wall: IF YOU EAT ANIMALS YOU CAN EAT ME, TOO. When Kurt is away or at lunch his colleagues often gossip about how to deal with the issue. Some of Kurt's colleagues don't really care, enjoying the edgy irreverence; others are offended by its brazen filth and inappropriateness. Harriet Graham is one of them. Though she loves animals, just recently a colleague educated her regarding the vague sexual reference buried in the statement. She has decided to inform Kurt of how she feels.

Harriet's Poorly Thought-Out Approach
Cubicle 35-R, Ninth Floor. 2:47 PM.

Harriet (tapping on Kurt's cubicle): Kurt, excuse me, please. Do you have a moment?

Kurt: Sure. What's shakin', Canadian bacon?

Harriet: Huh? Well, your little saying there about people eating animals and people . . . well . . . eating you.

Kurt: Yeah, what about it?

Harriet: I'm not sure that sort of . . . let's say . . . language is appropriate in a professional setting. Some might even consider it lewd.

Kurt: Lewd? Defending helpless animals from being eaten by overweight suburbanites is lewd? Harriet, I've seen you microwaving your frozen chicken dinners in the kitchen. Do you not think butchering, freezing, and heating an innocent chicken is lewd?

Harriet: Well, we all believe different things, Kurt. And we just have to accept that and be considerate of one another. But I think that your sign is very disrespectful to other employees. Especially our female colleagues.

Kurt: Disrespectful? I understand what you're saying, and I think you eating meat around me is disrespectful to me. Not to mention the dead chickens.

Harriet: Yes, Kurt. And I'm sorry if I offended you. But I think your stance on cruelty to animals could be better served by leaving out any sexual overtones. It may be attention grabbing, but in the end I think it turns people against your cause.

Kurt: There are no sexual overtones in my statement. By telling people they can "eat me" I mean it literally. They can eat me just like you eat microwaved chicken. Get your mind out of the gutter.

Harriet: That statement can be interpreted in many ways, and your choice is just one of them. We all know what you're trying to do.

Kurt: Well, it's not my problem if people like you with filthy minds misinterpret my sign.

Harriet: Ugh, honestly, Kurt. I give up. You're incorrigible.

Kurt: Meat is murder, Harriet. No matter how you freeze and package it. Someone has to fight the good fight.

Harriet's Well-Thought-Out Approach
Cubicle 35-R, Ninth Floor. 2:47 PM.

Harriet (tapping on Kurt's cubicle): Kurt, excuse me, please. Do you have a moment?

Kurt: Sure. What's shakin', Canadian bacon?

Harriet: I wanted you to know that I'm on my way to file a formal complaint against you at human resources citing sexual harassment. That sign of yours is demeaning, sexist, and lewd. It makes me feel exploited, threatened, and uncomfortable. I just wanted to give you a chance to apologize and remove the sign before I begin the process.

Kurt: I'm sorry, Harriet. Please don't file a complaint against me. I was just trying to get a rise out of people. You know, stir things up. Get some attention.

Harriet: Well, you got mine.

Kurt (standing up and taking down the sign): I really am sorry.

Harriet: Just be more considerate next time. And by the way, that little condescending shakin' and bacon rhyme you use instead of a normal greeting is very unprofessional. Particularly for someone who is against eating meat.

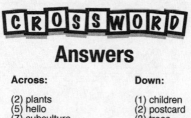

Answers

Across:

(2) plants
(5) hello
(7) subculture
(8) illicit
(11) famous
(12) personality
(14) driftwood
(16) fish
(17) glossy

Down:

(1) children
(2) postcard
(3) trees
(4) trip photos
(6) humor
(9) clothes
(10) bikini
(11) fy
(13) logo
(15) toga

Quick Quiz Self-Assessment

(1) Which of the following is not an appropriate bumper sticker to tack onto your cubicle wall?

    (a) I HIKED OLD RAG MOUNTAIN.

    (b) REPUBLICANS = WAR.

    (c) MY WIFE RAN AWAY WITH MY BEST FRIEND AND I SURE MISS HIM.

    (d) MUSICIANS ARE TUNED IN.

(2) True or False? A good way for shy employees to introduce themselves to their colleagues is by decorating their cubicles with personal but inoffensive objects and photos.

(3) Identify the most appropriate decoration for your cubicle:
    (a) Saltwater aquarium.
    (b) Small, shade-loving flower.
    (c) Home stereo system.
    (d) Dallas Cowboy cheerleaders poster.

ANSWERS:
(1) b, c. (2) True. (3) b.

CHAPTER THREE

On the Phone

When America's founding fathers penned the US Constitution and the Bill of Rights, they had no idea that one day entire generations of Americans would spend most of their productive years crowded into tiny spaces beneath glaring lights divided by carpeted walls. Forget the Patriot Act; how many rights to privacy and self-expression do we forfeit for the sake of corporate political correctness, institutionalized homogeneity, and a secure paycheck? Live free or die, but whatever you do—don't rock the company boat with personal or embarrassing information. Not if you want to sail in the seas of steady income and health insurance. Never raise your voice on the phone, and always remember that the speakerphone is for conferences, not one-on-one conversations. Don't forget where you are.

Exercising your right to privacy (not to mention freedom of speech) is a difficult, if not costly, proposition in corporate environments. Nevertheless, there will come a time when you will be forced to discuss your health and deeply personal information while at your cubicle. Other than salary, the reason you put up with your job is because of full dental plus low deductibles and co-payments. You will use these benefits, so be prepared to discuss the results.

Explaining Ailments to the Doctor

Talking with your doctor on the phone in your cubicle is, of course, a last resort. But there are times when anxiety and schedules make it the only option. So when you're discussing your health or other sensitive content, use highly specialized questions and answers. Don't discuss illnesses, diseases, or other personal problems by name if it isn't necessary. Your co-workers, bosses, and colleagues do not want to overhear that you've entered menopause, have a gambling addiction, are pregnant, or have contracted an itchy fungus between your toes. Have the person on the other side of the conversation do the talking; he or she is the one with all the information. The key to privatizing your cubicle discourse is to ask general questions and respond with one-word answers. Be careful with your diction (word choice), phrasing, and sentence structure. Use the filter in your head. Do not ask questions impulsively or answer them emotionally. Your professional life is listening.

SAMPLE CONVERSATIONS

Bad Choice of Language
Cubicle 87-N, Second Floor. 4:33 PM.

Doctor: The nurse told me the symptoms you've been experiencing, and I think I have the answer for you.

You: Do I have hemorrhoids? Damn! I knew it. I feel like I'm sitting on a campfire.

Doctor: Yes.

You: Oh my God. What kind of medication do you recommend? I hope not some smelly cream. That stuff makes me nauseous.

Doctor: I recommend applying a new odorless ointment called Hyposoapitan.

You: That sounds expensive. Does my insurance cover problems with my rectum?

(Everyone around you begins sending e-mails to their office mates.)

Excellent Choice of Language
Cubicle 87-N, Second Floor. 4:33 PM.

Doctor: The nurse told me the symptoms you've been experiencing, and I think I have the answer for you.

You: Great! Got any specifics?

Doctor: The discomfort you've been experiencing is from hemorrhoids.

You: Thanks for that information. What's the next step?

Doctor: I recommend treating it with this new odorless ointment called Hyposoapitan.

You: Okay, thanks again. Let me look into the specifics and I'll get back to you if I have any questions.

(All those around you have already tuned you out, but they are nevertheless glad you are off the phone and no longer talking about whatever it was you were talking about.)

Dealing with the Significant Other

Love may be blind, but the people you work with can see how you are acting. They can hear you, too. Everyone knows you love your spouse; that's why you got married. Congratulations on your good fortune. There is nothing wrong with telling someone you love him or her—in your bed. You don't wear your pajamas or discuss personal finances at work for a reason. Certain things are better done and *said* at home. This advice may sound conservative and uptight, but so are neckties, high heels, and ID cards. The corporation is not a place of intimacy. Yet it is also not an emotional slaughterhouse. So learn where to draw the line. A quick "I love you" is acceptable if you are hanging up the phone or if your significant other is about to go away on a business trip. A prolonged "I love you" is an effusive expression of emotion masking amazement that someone in the world would actually care about you.

If you and your significant other walk through the park with your hands in each other's back pockets, kiss on the escalator, or trade winks across the Thanksgiving dinner table, chances are you aren't the type of people who hide or perhaps even filter your feelings in public. However, public displays of affection at work, particularly over the telephone, are more inappropriate and annoying than you may think—and for good reason. Your co-workers, colleagues, and bosses will know when there are problems in loveland. If you choose to emote over the work phone, prepare yourself for the consequences.

Any change in conversational tone, style, length, or, of course, diction is the same as turning around, facing your work neighbors, and saying clearly through a construction cone, "I'm not going to tell my wife I love her today because I'm impotent and she's venting her frustration by calling my mother an ice witch." Given the opportunity, the imaginations of those around you will run free like wild horses across the prairies of your touchy-feely relationship. So if you catch your husband in the back of your SUV with your neighbor's cheerleader daughter, be prepared to tell him you love him when he calls you at work asking for forgiveness—that is, unless you want everyone to know you're lovingly married to a man who cheats with pom-pom girls. Ignoring a ringing phone eight inches from your elbow is unprofessional and the hallmark of an employee trying to avoid contact with a client or customer. When in doubt, hang up and find an alternate phone. Hanging up says a lot more and a lot less than trying to whisper your way through a heated argument or faking an emotional state that will only cause you to wreck your car on the way home.

SAMPLE CONVERSATIONS

Bad Choice of Language
Cubicle 44-W, Twelfth Floor. 9:33 AM.

Significant Other: Honey, I'm so sorry about cheating with my sales representative. She means nothing to me. It's just that you and I have been drifting apart. With your working and my job, we just don't spend time together anymore. Not just time, but quality time. I've felt so alone recently. I've felt unloved and unwanted for weeks. No, months.

You (muffling the phone with tightly gripped hands): Well, you should have said something before fu . . . meeting that . . . after the shareholders' conference. You should have thought about me, about us, first.

By the way, I'm working because *we*, not *I*, need the money.

Significant Other: I know, honey. It's not your fault. We're just doing our best to make ends meet. To make lives for ourselves. That's why it's so hard to believe that that's the exact thing that drove us apart. Let's start this whole thing over. Let's begin again and focus on *us* this time. No more fights about money and expenses and savings. Only talks about us and what we're going to do so this never happens again. We've got too much to lose to let this break us apart. I'm so sorry, honey. Please come home so we can fix things.

You (muffling phone with sweaty hands): Well, ah, I've got a lot to do. I don't think I can ever . . . We'll talk when I get home.

Significant Other: I love you.

You (easing grip on phone and saying for those around you to hear): *I love you, too.*

(No one notices the fight you just had. Yet they do notice the outline of your bra because your sweat-drenched white blouse is stuck to your back.)

Excellent Choice of Language
Cubicle 44-W, Twelfth Floor. 9:33 AM.

Significant Other: Honey, I'm so sorry about cheating with my sales representative. She means nothing to me. It's just that you and I have been drifting apart. With your working and my job, we just don't spend time together anymore. Not just time, but quality

Fixing General Messes on the Phone

CUBE TIP

Set up your phone so that the ringer is on mute but the ID display is clearly in your field of sight. This way you can screen your calls without anyone else knowing.

As we have learned, public displays of affection in the office are inappropriate simply because professionalism means being able to put the corporate objective above everything else, including your personal life. Likewise, don't try to resolve personal problems at the office, especially in your cubicle. Despite what you may want to believe, you are not being paid to be in a cubicle—you are being paid to work. So limit your non-work-related calls as much as possible. The spouses of US Marines do not call their significant others during operations to complain about a broken toilet, their recent and suspicious aloofness, or dirty dishes in the sink. They know that professional soldiers jeopardize the mission and safety of their colleagues if their personal lives enter their professional lives. As a professional, you're not any different. So take control of your anger, frustration, or disappointment by scheduling an appointment to meet it. Get together for coffee later. Establish a good time to return the call when you have privacy. Take a walk around the building and figure out a game plan. Don't make calls or answer them impulsively. And don't indulge people who can't understand your need to act like a professional at work.

Gabbing with Friends and Colleagues on the Phone

So you got laid. Well done. Yes, given that she was willing to sleep with you on the first date, I think she'll return your call. If she calls while you're gone, have one of your colleagues answer the phone: They know all the details of the "tagging" anyway. Who needs to confide in friends when the details of your life are public information? Perhaps Veronica from last night has a friend; Joshua, who works two cubes away, hasn't had any action in months. Speaking of Joshua, Evelyn overheard him saying that he got a raise by just asking for it. He told Stephen over in accounting that his boss is a sucker for sob stories, particularly ones that involve overtime and sick grandmothers. In six days this information makes it back to Joshua's boss and Joshua gets canned. Now not even Veronica would want to go out with him.

Be careful. Friends and close colleagues have a way of lulling employees into a false sense of uninhibited comfort. Acting and talking with your friends and colleagues as if you're at Starbucks can inadvertently invite the entire office into your bedroom and bank account. If you aren't willing to share both with your co-workers, hang up and meet your friends somewhere down the street for a beer.

Yo Entiendo

Gone are the days when you could share your deepest secrets in Pig Latin and render your parents oblivious to the fact that you licked pine tree bark in an attempt to get sick and miss fourth grade. However, grown-ups in the cubicle community who speak a second language have a similar opportunity to converse without having to edit their words or camouflage their emotions. Yet, like Pig Latin, more and more Americans speak second languages, especially Spanish. Bilingual and multilingual cubicle dwellers should therefore be careful when they decide to transition into a language other than English on the company telephone. Like it or not, business is probably conducted in the English language in your cubicle community. So accept the reality that most co-workers and superiors assume you are not talking about work when you stray from speaking English. Just because those around can't understand what you are saying doesn't mean they can't understand what you are doing.

Whether you are speaking in Armenian, Chinese, or English, when you're talking with friends and family on the company phone and on company time, do it in moderation. Nothing indicates a lack of professionalism more than not caring about how you are perceived by your colleagues. So keep in mind that some employees and bosses become irritated by having to listen to a cubicle neighbor ramble on and on in a language they don't understand. Invariably, when people cannot understand what is being said around them, they for some masochistic reason attempt to interpret what is being said by deciphering the speaker's inflection, tone, and other characteristics of the conversation.

English	Chinese	Japanese	Spanish	Russian	French	Pig Latin
cheapskate	tschiou	kechinbou	tacaño	скряга	économique	eapskatechay
idiot	bai tschi	baka	idiota	идиот	imbécile	idiotway
lush	joyou goi	yopparai	borracho	пышный	alcoolique	ushlay
moron	jiu jung	teinousha	tonto	идиот	crétin fini	oronmay
slut	beiou tzu	yariman	una cua	неряха	salope	utslay
womanizer	dung tu tzu	jigoro	mujeriego	бабник	salope	omanizerway

As cubicle residents across America listen to their neighbors speak in Arabic, Spanish, Thai, Portuguese, French, Vietnamese, or any language that they don't comprehend, they all come to the same conclusion: *I think they're talking about me. Did I hear my name? Why are they laughing? Was my zipper down this morning?* So before the situation devolves into misunderstandings and accusations, cubicle inhabitants of all backgrounds and language abilities can do themselves and their colleagues a favor by simply limiting the amount of non-business-related phone conversations. The one Albanian in your cubicle neighborhood shouldn't feel he has a free pass to seduce his ex-girlfriend for thirty minutes on his work phone simply because no one around him can understand what he is saying.

Your colleagues are smart, and—even more disturbing—they're curious. So if you wouldn't have the conversation in English, don't have it in another language. Besides, judging people works both ways. Don't assume the new co-worker two cubicles away is saying bad things about you in Spanish. And don't assume the new co-worker two cubicles away doesn't understand Spanish.

Never Whisper

Just as speaking a foreign language for an extended duration makes others speculate as to what is being discussed, nothing creates an aura of gossip more than whispering. Yet it happens all the time, every day, in every cubicle community. Don't think your colleagues aren't paying attention to your phone conversation. They are. Especially when the voice level suddenly changes or there is an obvious alteration in inflection. Most cubicle phone conversations begin at a normal voice level, or the "hushed" voice level common to polite cubicle banter; the hushed cubicle voice resembles the volume people use in the library. Inevitably, however, conversations between colleagues, friends, or family members swirl into personal realms, and these areas often involve the people we work with. By speaking at a normal level, and then dropping into a whisper to conceal a name, a revealing detail, or sensitive issue, you are not fooling anyone. Even worse, you are stoking the fiery imaginations of human beings forced to sit at a desk surrounded by fabric walls. You may not be talking about them, but their imaginations don't know that. Also, by sitting in a cubicle yourself, it is impossible for you to know who is passing by or quietly standing nearby searching their pockets for their ID card. They may think you know they're there and so you are whispering. For instance, who wouldn't think the following conversation might be about them:

> **Employee:** Girl, you're not gonna believe what Tanya said about *whisper.* Everyone in the company knows except *whisper.* Isn't that crazy? The only person who doesn't know is the one everyone is laughing at! I'm glad I'm not *whisper.* I guess he'll never try to get a date in this city again!

Or this phone conversation:

> **Employee:** Dude, did you hear about that picture of *whisper* getting e-mailed around the office? It's hysterical! Evidently it was taken on a camera cell phone while she had no idea anyone was looking. If *whisper* ever found out, she would die from embarrassment. She always acts like she's so freaking professional and prudish. I guess that is the last time *whisper* will ever do that. Hold on, I'm e-mailing to your personal address now.

Or this one:

> **Employee:** *Whisper, whisper, whisper, whisper, whisper,* just last week, *whisper, whisper, whisper,* I know! *Whisper, whisper, whisper.*

Interrupting Phone Calls

There's no reason not to know when a colleague is on the phone. Cubicles were designed specifically for these types of situations—so everyone knows what everyone else is doing. Don't tap on a colleague's cubicle and begin the conversation with, "Oh, are you on the phone?" Before you even begin tapping or before you announce your arrival, check to make sure the person you are about to engage is not already engaged in some other activity, such as talking on the phone with an important client. If someone you need to talk with is speaking with someone else on the phone, simply walk back to your cubicle, make a maintenance trip to the bathroom, go visit another colleague, or find something productive to do. Do not stand at your co-worker's back or hover in the vicinity. Such behavior is passive-aggressive and the sign of someone who lacks patience and respect for their colleagues' time and other responsibilities.

Message Maintenance

Your voice-mail message is the first real contact many of your clients or customers will have with you. Don't take this first impression for granted. Your message is important; those who listen to it will immediately begin to speculate what you look, act, and dress like. So make sure the tone of your voice, the words you choose, and the message you leave are professional, polite, and sincere. Don't use gimmicky slogans or obsequious declarations such as "Your call is important to me." Of course their call should be important to you. Actually saying this belittles customers and implies that you think they should be grateful for your services. Remember, they are paying your company. They do not want to hear that they're important. How patronizing. That should be a given. It's the same as when elementary schools put signs around the property informing people that they are in a DRUG-FREE ZONE. Really? How nice. I thought all elementary schools are supposed to be drug-free zones. Thank you for the information. And by the way, what everyone already knows is that just because you claim something is true doesn't mean it *is* true. In fact, if you tell people your call is important to them or that there are no drugs in an elementary school, most people are inclined to raise an eyebrow and assume they are being lied to. Anyone who chooses to point out what is normally already assumed should be considered suspicious. Don't leave a voice-mail message that evokes suspicion.

What customers really want is for you to pick up the phone and do what they are paying your company to do. If you aren't there, you're already one step behind. So if you are going on vacation or will be away from the office, leave information that will be as helpful as possible to callers in light of your absence. First, tell them how long you will be gone and when you will return. That way customers, clients, and colleagues are clear on your schedule and can plan their requests, schedules, or questions accordingly.

Most callers will work with your schedule. We all understand the need for vacations and time away. Being away from your desk is not unprofessional. Being away from your desk and not providing callers with helpful information is very unprofessional. After providing the details of your time away, give callers options. Tell them right away that if there's an emergency, they can call one of your colleagues whom you know will be at the office.

Leave your co-worker's number and speak slowly and clearly while doing so. Furnish customers with other helpful resources that may answer general inquiries, such as the front desk number or company website address. That's it. That's all you need to do. If you are one those people who feels it necessary to apologize for not being able to take the call, go ahead. But don't go any further than that. Anything beyond the necessary information and a quick apology for the inconvenience is overkill.

Example of a Bad Voice-Mail Message
Cubicle 9-B, Twenty-fourth Floor. 4:05 PM.

Sales Client: Hello?

Sales Representative: Hi! You've reached Kendra Boone, image marketing representative at Cubers International. Unfortunately, I'm unable to take your call right now because my boyfriend and I are going to France! Your call is very, very important to me, so please leave a message at the beep and I'll get back to you as soon as possible! Bon voyage!

Sales Client: *Click.*

Sales Client (two minutes later): Hello? Public Perception Incorporated? I was wondering if you could process a rush promotions makeover. It's a big one.

Example of a Good Voice-Mail Message
Cubicle 9-B, Twenty-fourth Floor. 4:05 PM.

Sales Client: Hello?

Sales Representative: Hi, you've reached Kendra Boone at Cubers International. Unfortunately, I'm

unable to take your call because I will be out of the
office from Monday, February 21, through Friday,
February 25. If you need immediate assistance,
please contact my colleague Dustin Glennon at
716-555-8919. Otherwise please leave a message or
call back upon my return next Monday. Thank you.
Sales Client: *Click.*
Sales Client (two minutes later): Hello? Dustin
Glennon? I was wondering if you could process a
rush order. It's a big one.

Follow the Corporate Script

I t is easy for cubicle residents to feel too comfortable with
their jobs and clients over time, especially when speaking on
the phone. Such a drop in professional formality is normally
a multifaceted process. After several months employees don't
dress as well. Instead of beginning work at 9 AM, they arrive at
9:15. Some begin to treat their professional colleagues as personal friends and converse with them in informal language
during important meetings, or even drop in a profane word
every now and then. Managers do their best to keep up morale,
but it's up to individual employees to take care of themselves
and keep a vigilant eye on their professional standards. Other
than upsetting their bosses directly, the most common mistake
employees make is taking their relationships with clients for
granted. Always remember: It's business. So when you see your
favorite customer's number appear on your company's caller
ID, don't scoop up the phone and blurt, "Hey, you! How's it
going?" No matter how friendly your business relationship becomes, it never evolves to the point that it's not about business.
When you answer the company phone, do it in your company

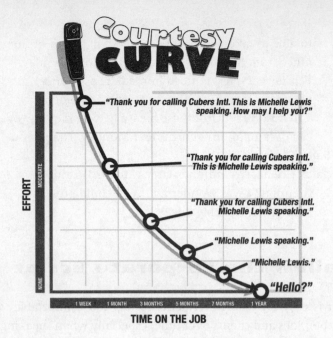

Courtesy CURVE

EFFORT (MODERATE / NONE)

"Thank you for calling Cubers Intl. This is Michelle Lewis speaking. How may I help you?"

"Thank you for calling Cubers Intl. This is Michelle Lewis speaking."

"Thank you for calling Cubers Intl. Michelle Lewis speaking."

"Michelle Lewis speaking."

"Michelle Lewis."

"Hello?"

1 WEEK   1 MONTH   3 MONTHS   5 MONTHS   7 MONTHS   1 YEAR

TIME ON THE JOB

voice, and follow the company script. Most corporations simply tell employees how to answer the phone on the first day. As time passes, however, our phone manners tend to deteriorate.

Resist the temptation to become lazy regarding your phone manners. The company script will seem impersonal and robotic even after a few days, but by making it a habit you will always err on the side of caution. Informality is great for making clients and customers feel as if they know you. Informality is horrible for making clients and customers feel as if they can trust you.

Speakerphone Divas

After experimenting with the speakerphone a few times, many employees have difficulty weaning themselves off it. Their addiction, however, is understandable. The speaker-phone makes us feel powerful, loved, and part of something exciting. How many opportunities does regular life allow for being able to speak to more than one person, if not dozens of people, on the phone at the same time? On speakerphone you have an audience. After a while employees can't go for long without feeling like a celebrity. They become speaker-phone divas. They need the rush of being on the speakerphone stage, where they dispense advice, crack bad jokes, and take control as if they

INSENSITIVE
SPEAKER

are running their own concert tour. Speakerphone divas be-come overwhelmed by their own imaginations. Many stop using the receiver altogether, thinking it a proletarian vice. As they spiral down their slippery slope, speakerphone divas be-come detached from the realities of the cubicle community. Un-fortunately, in the politically correct and sensitive corporate environment it is impossible for an employee, or even groups of employees, to tell others like these divas how to do their jobs. The conversation can quickly devolve into an acrimonious de-bate about work ethics and personal sensibilities.

Speakerphone divas have a very low recovery rate and often live in denial for their entire careers. They become so self-absorbed and oblivious to humanity that they begin to think like those Adonis cycling addicts who wear spandex shorts and ergonomic water backpacks, and have the audacity to complain about actual cars driving on roads. You've seen these crazed cyclists—the ones who scream at motorists as if the narrow stretch of pavement leading into the city were constructed for them and their two-ounce bicycles alone. They view car people as unhealthy and overweight polluters of the environment. Likewise, speakerphone divas loathe regular phone users. They regard regular phone users as menial brutes with bent necks and dirty hands. Trying to change the mind of a speakerphone diva is, like cycling on a busy road, an exercise in frustration.

Cell Phone

Just as the Internet saved cubicle employees from infinite boredom, the cell phone has saved them from infinite exposure. No longer is it considered inappropriate to make a fake trip to the photocopier to use your cell phone. Yes, e-mail and instant messages are great for general entertainment, making jokes, and slogging gossip, but sometimes life requires a real conversation. Only the voice of a trusted friend, lover, or family member can save a relationship, thwart an anxiety attack, or shine light on a dark bout of depression. But remember to keep your ringer off. Track your cell phone's incoming calls by setting it to vibrate or muting it and discreetly keeping it next to your keyboard. Everyone in your cubicle neighborhood knows what their colleagues are doing when their cell phones ring and they suddenly make a trip to the bathroom. Why take an unnecessary hit to your work-ethic reputation? By quietly monitoring your incoming cell-phone calls, you can leave your cubicle to return them with no one the wiser. And don't be naïve: Cubicle communities are self-monitoring entities. Everyone knows the guy who goes to the bathroom suspiciously often or the crazy woman who takes a cell-phone break every twenty minutes to check on her boyfriend after finding out he cheated on her last year. Protect your reputation by silencing your cell phone and changing your call location every two days.

Quick Quiz Self-Assessment

(1) Complete the following phone sentence with the most appropriate word(s). "I'm sorry, but I'm not free to discuss this now. I _____

    (a) can't stand you."

    (b) don't think about you."

    (c) will call you later."

    (d) have a date with the sales representative."

(2) Finish the following phone conversation with the most appropriate response.

Caller: Your son has been picked up by the police. Please come to the station as soon as you can to pick him up.

    (a) I'm going to kill that kid. Is he on drugs again?

    (b) Thank you for the phone call. I'm leaving in a few minutes and will call you from my cell phone.

    (c) How in the hell do you think I can make it to the police station when my boss won't even let me off early on Christmas Eve?

    (d) You have the wrong number.

(3) True or False? Talking to your doctor on the phone in your cubicle should be standard practice because everyone understands your situation and if you muffle your voice they won't hear you anyway.

ANSWERS:

(1) c. (2) b. (3) False. Speaking with your doctor while in your cubicle should be avoided at all costs. If you must, however, use general language so as not to divulge specifics. Muffling your voice will only lead to speculation and gossip, particularly if this is not your normal method of operation.

CHAPTER FOUR

Illness, Body Functions, and Injuries

Every professional knows that sick days are not days for being sick; they are days for calling in sick. Savvy business people know who they are: They know their own hearts, they know their own minds, they know their own immune systems. If you get the flu every year and have fourteen days of sick leave, factor in five sick days for being legitimately sick, plus four more for other ailments such as bad colds, general depression, and a twisted ankle. The remaining five days are, of course, "sick of work" vacation days. Though using these sick days forces you to lie to your boss and maybe even fake a lingering cough when you return, the benefits far outweigh the risks.

Sure, you may go to Hell, or whatever version of Hell you believe in, if you lie. If you don't lie, however, you are most certainly going to be stuck in your cubicle. Another given in life is that you will die someday. So take your sick leave and use it to take your stalled marriage to a bed-and-breakfast. Paint your bland apartment orange. Practice your shoddy Hungarian. Pilates your triceps. Ponder a lonely painting in an empty museum. Play air guitar in a funeral home parking lot. Do anything that contributes to fulfillment in your life. Call in sick and go out and live. If you must answer your cell phone, remember not to overact the symptoms of your infirmity, but sniffle or cough every several minutes, even if you're on a roller coaster.

Managing the Symptoms, Not the Disease

To free up the "sick of work" vacation days, you may have to go to work on days when you're actually sick. No matter how many symptoms are pouring from your nose, eyes, ears, and mouth, if you want that extra time next week to spend with your nose-ring girlfriend at the twenty-four-hour poetry slamfest you must never admit to being sick at work. Your colleagues know this game, but they also know when people are pushing the limits too far and living on the edge of contagion. If you freely admit to being unwell, co-workers will see the disease and not the patient. So be assertive about your good health. If you love your girlfriend, you are "good, but not 100 percent" or "a little under the weather" or "have allergies" or "fine, but feeling run-down" or "stressed about work and didn't sleep last night." Try to characterize your undeniable symptoms—coughing, sneezing, runny nose, swollen red eyes—as somehow being work related. No one has sympathy for a person who gets a bad cold from a borrowed set of golf clubs. Stay on message.

> ### Tom's Good Attempt to Manage the Symptoms
> #### Cubicle 11-J, Thirty-first Floor. 3:34 PM.
>
> **Tom's Colleague:** Hey, Tom. Are you okay? Your nose is red and your eyes are all puffy. You're not sick, are you?

Tom: Me? Oh, no. Gosh, do I look sick? You know, I've been so stressed out about getting this report done that I haven't really been sleeping well. I'm burning the candle at both ends to impress this new client. No big deal. Things will settle down when we have vacation next December.

Tom's Colleague (calling his boss): Hey, Mary. I spoke with Amanda over at McCloy and Burnham and they said the Cubers International order was fine. The problem they had with shipping was with another provider. By the way, what's up with Tom? He looks like he may be sick.

Tom's Boss (calling Tom): Hey, Tom. Mary. Thanks for your work on the new client in Minneapolis. They seem very happy. Hope they're not driving you too crazy. By the way, are you okay? I hear you're sick?

Tom: Thanks, Mary. No. I'm not sick. I'm just a little run-down. No such thing as a second first impression with a new client. But I'm fine. Thanks for asking.

Tom's Boss: Good to hear. But don't work too hard. Take a day or two off if you need it.

Tom (leaving a message on his girlfriend's answering machine—on his cell phone during lunch, of course): Hey, babe. Miss you tons. But next Friday works perfectly. We can probably park behind the coffeehouse, between the Dumpsters. (Beat boxing slam poetry) I love you like a steam train off da track / I give you my love / you give it back / we both feeling whack. Peace out, babe.

Sneezing is a form of assault, and those who have not been taught or figured out how to cover their noses and mouths are a threat to everyone around them. Some think turning their head away is enough, others believe deflecting the snot spray with a flattened hand is ample prevention, and there are those who don't seem to care at all. Co-workers know the sound and duration of unregulated sneezes—they're as fluid as a golf swing and as wet as a lawn sprinkler. Bad sneezers belong in quarantine rooms in underground laboratories, not cubicles. Stay away from them. You can identify bad sneezers' cubicles because the unfettered blast of saliva and mucous splatters onto their computer monitor illuminating it like a bad LiteBrite pattern. Sneezing, however, is just the beginning. Soiled tissues are equally menacing. Buy a box of tissues and keep it on your desk. Throw used tissues away immediately. Don't substitute a box of tissues with real-time options such as toilet paper stolen from the company bathroom or the paper towel you wrapped your morning muffin in.

Unprepared sneezers often abuse a single ball of toilet paper or paper towel sheet for hours, sneezing into it, probing their nostrils with it, and wiping down their hands. Eventually this option becomes too trodden, weak, and soggy for further use. Nevertheless, there are those in your cubicle farm who will refuse to replace it and will, with pinched fingers, gently spread it out like a spiderweb before blowing their noses with it, sneezing toxins through it onto their own

CUBE TIP

Make frequent, but discreet trips (use detours, misdirection) to the bathroom to treat the symptoms of your illness. Sometimes a few shots of nose spray, drops of Visine, and a good nose clearing in an anonymous bathroom stall can give you hours of healthy demeanor.

diseased hands. These same people have a habit of leaving the fibrous clump of germs near their keyboards for emergencies. Avoid shaking hands with bad sneezers. If necessary, drop whatever you're holding and immediately steer the conversation beyond pleasantries while in the squatting position. If your office features a holiday-season gift exchange, nothing says *I love you, co-worker* more than an entire plastic-wrapped pallet of tissue boxes. Being prepared is the first rule to managing symptoms.

CUBICLE FIRST-AID KIT: The same people who have a post-nuclear-bomb-detonation basement stocked full of duct tape, canned soup, water purification tablets, Ace bandages, dried fruits, defibrillators, powdered milk, and extra-strength aspirin, work at a desk with only old gum wrappers, stray pennies, pen tops, and crusty rubber bands in the drawers. Why? Because being vaporized is scarier than having a paper cut bleed all over the Anderson contract. Which is more likely? On any given day, who knows. Which do you have more control over? The paper cut. So be responsible. Always have an ample supply of Band-Aids, Visine, cough drops, nose spray, aspirin, Handi Wipes, tweezers, and throat lozenges in case of small emergencies. Colleagues never forget who gave them a Band-Aid for a bloody hangnail or a couple of aspirin for a work-induced headache. Helping co-workers in their time of need is a step toward becoming professionally and socially indispensable.

Managing the Disease, Not the Symptoms

Boxing referees, nurses, welders, doctors, cafeteria ladies, hockey players, Southern debutantes, beekeepers, and oyster shuckers all wear gloves to protect themselves from occupational and environmental hazards. In the office, however, wearing gloves is inappropriate because it implies that your co-workers and environment are unsanitary, diseased, even dangerous. Nevertheless, employees in cubicle farms often transmit colds, influenza, gastrointestinal illnesses, and other communicable diseases from one person to the next because they share the same air, office supplies, doorknobs, and kitchen amenities. What can you do to defend yourself against the constant barrage of germs and contagions in the workplace? Plenty. Begin by protecting your hands. (Note: There is no substitute for washing your hands thoroughly with soap and water.) Keep an alcohol-based hand sanitizer in your cubicle, preferably in a drawer. This way none of your colleagues will "borrow" it and you won't come across as a Howard Hughes paranoid phobic. Next, germ-proof your computer keyboard. Use cotton swabs and/or cotton balls dampened with isopropyl alcohol to clean the individual keys and exterior contours. Then wipe the keyboard clean with a lint-free cloth. (It's also a good idea to use compressed air or a mini vacuum to rid your keyboard of dust, hair, food particles, and other unsavory elements beneath the keys. Some people even wash their keyboards in the dishwasher, but keyboards take days to dry; if yours is that soiled, request a new one from your IT department.)

Next, thoroughly clean your mouse and phone with cotton balls and isopropyl alcohol. It's also a good idea to clean your desktop area routinely with a fresh cloth and antibacterial cleaner. Examine your environment. Make sure there is proper lighting in and around your cubicle so your eyes aren't strained or blinded by unhealthy amounts of light. Stay out of the path of air-conditioning vents and other climate-control apertures so that you aren't exposed to abrupt, feverish fluctuations in temperature and humidity. Your cubicle isn't very formidable; with proper planning and supplies, however, you can make it a daunting perimeter between you and the germs you work near.

Hangovers

Also known in medical circles as "Brown Bottle Flu," hangovers are politically incorrect; there isn't an employee in the Budweiser headquarters who would openly admit to being hungover on a Tuesday. Nevertheless, alcohol is an institution among the cubicle class, like Febreze, but for the soul. From casual drinkers to functional alcoholics, most cubicle dwellers have been hung over at work, yet sometimes identifying the difference between hangovers and other illnesses such as colds and flu is difficult. So examine your co-workers carefully. Cold and flu sufferers are lethargic, but hungover colleagues actively avoid contact with others for fear of being outed. They have hangover paranoia, which is largely the fear of smelling like alcohol. People suffering from hangover paranoia walk briskly but painfully down hallways to reduce casual-encounter opportunities. They hibernate in their cubicles and drink water by the gulp. They breathe lightly and, during conversations, tilt their heads at odd angles, often at their shoes, so they don't project alcohol fumes. Other telltale hangover symptoms include bloodshot and baggy eyes, an anguished lack of focus, a pained sense of passing time, and wearing the same clothes they wore yesterday.

God Bless You?

Do you say "Bless you" when your neighbor sneezes? What about when *his* neighbor sneezes? Such seemingly mundane and innocuous situations have perplexed cubicle dwellers since the Atari 1200. Yet, as with civilization itself, the collective rules of behavior on the cubicle farm are in a constant state of flux. Generally, if your neighbors sneeze, you are

BATHR🚹🚺M RUN!

Not feeling 100 percent? Better navigate through your cubicle farm as quickly as you can.

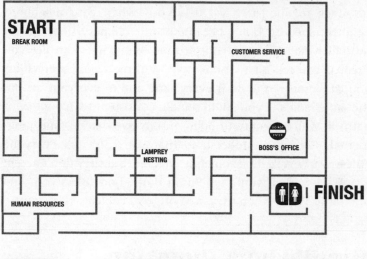

YOUR AILMENT	TIME TO BEAT	YOUR TIME
COMMON COLD	9 sec	
INFLUENZA	11 sec	
VIRAL INFECTION	22 sec	
HANGOVER	31 sec	

obligated to say "Bless you." Why? Because it's a polite way of acknowledging your neighbors' suffering, and small acts of decency are the cornerstone of humanity. Also, it informs neighbors that you are indeed paying attention to their illness and they had better not get you sick. Keep in mind, however, that the modern workplace is a sophisticated blend of different cultures, perspectives, and beliefs. So whenever possible, keep any reference to your religious affiliations to yourself. By simply saying "Bless you," you are really saying, *I'm paranoid about offending you and don't know if by saying "God" or "Allah" or "Buddha" you will become angry and insulted. So I'm going to play it safe and be politically correct. Bless you.* Your neighbors should immediately dispense of used tissue and respectfully reply, "Thank you." Communication complete; no one got hurt. You are not, however, required to say "Bless you" when your neighbor's neighbor sneezes. This is because of the "slippery-slope" factor by which failing to set conspicuous boundaries can get you fired. If you tell a co-worker two or three cubes over "Bless you," be prepared to do it every time and to everyone within the same radius. If you fail to remain consistent with your sympathies, you are guilty of being insensitive, biased, and judgmental. Colleagues understand that you can't tell everyone "Bless you" every time someone sneezes, but they don't accept why a co-worker would tell Susan Hammond "Bless you" and not Samir Pasha when they are both two cubicles away.

The Obvious Question

There are times in the cubicle community when a co-worker shows up with a swollen eye, a broken leg, or a sprained finger wrapped in a splint and elastic bandage. These occasions leave everyone awkward because, of course, the thought in everyone's mind is *What happened?* In theory, when it comes to injuries, ailments, and most other sickly symptoms, corporations have quietly adopted the ubiquitous *Don't ask, don't tell* policy that turns otherwise apathetic people into gossip-mongers and amateur J. Edgar Hoovers. *Don't ask, don't tell* is just another bureaucratic way of saying, *Nothing to see here.* Unfortunately, not asking and not telling does nothing to curb people from wanting to know. So on days when the habitually quiet and reserved employee shows up with a black eye and broken hand, it is the injured person's duty to put all inquiring minds at ease. Of course, this becomes difficult if the story behind the injury involves a bar fight, a lovers' spat, or an act of such stupidity that one's reputation at work would incur irreversible damage. So how do you explain an embarrassing or too-personal injury? Answer: With spin. If you were intelligent enough and socially adept enough to outcompete several prospective employees in a series of interviews, then you should have the skills to be able to handle an unexpected reputation crisis at work. The trick is to behave like a politician and answer all questions without actually answering a single one of them.

Bad Attempt to Spin an Injury on Monday Morning
Cubicle 66-R, Sixth Floor. 10:01 AM.

Nosy Employee: Oh my God! Marcus! What happened to your eye?

Marcus: Nothing. What are you . . . Oh, you mean this shiner? Is it that noticeable?

Nosy Employee: Noticeable? You look like you got in a fight with a silverback gorilla wielding a nine iron!

Marcus: Just don't say anything to anyone. I don't want you pointing it out to other people. I'm hoping they won't notice it. You know, I sit in my cube most of the day.

Nosy Employee: Are you kidding me? The only person who isn't going to notice that is Harold, and that's because he's on vacation for three weeks in Italy. And that's assuming he doesn't look west.

Marcus: Okay, okay. Just don't tell anyone. I got in a fight Saturday night. I was pretty drunk and this guy said my girlfriend was a slut.

Nosy Employee: You don't have a girlfriend, man. You just got divorced last week.

Marcus: I know, but from what I remember she was pretty hot. And she was being nice to me. She even touched my arm and said I was funny. In my mind I kind of thought she might be my girlfriend in the future.

Nosy Employee: Hilarious! Did you ever stop to think that maybe she *was* a slut? Hell, she could have even been a dude, man. Holy crap! Wait until this gets around the office.

Marcus: Just don't tell anyone.

Nosy Employee: Oh sure, man. I'm not going to say a word. Anyway, you might want to put some ice on that. It looks like there might be some pus seeping out of there. Um, I've got some e-mails to answer. Let me know if you need anything.

Good Attempt to Spin an Injury on Monday Morning
Cubicle 66-R, Sixth Floor. 10:01 AM.

Nosy Employee: Oh my God! Marcus! What happened to your eye?

Marcus: Well, I got in a fight defending an acquaintance of mine. She was really being screwed with by some asshole at the bar. He was calling her all sorts of terrible things. And, well, sometimes you just have to protect people from aggressors.

Nosy Employee: No way, man! Did you get a good shot in? You know, most people around here wouldn't stir things up to save their lives. You're a rebel, man. That's totally badass.

Marcus: Yeah, sometimes you just have to put yourself in the line of fire to protect those who can't defend themselves. Even if that means putting your own life at risk.

Nosy Employee: That's awesome. You're the very definition of a hero. Is it okay if I tell others what happened to you? I want to respect your privacy, but let's face it, everyone is going to ask what happened.

Marcus: Well, the story is going to get out. Just try not to exaggerate and make me into some kind of hero. You know that's not how I roll. Besides, you would have done the same thing in my position.

Nosy Employee: Sure, man. Of course I would have done the same thing. We get each other. We're the same type of people.

Marcus: Thanks for understanding.

Nosy Employee: You got it. Maybe we can hang next weekend.

Marcus: Sure, buddy. Anyway, I've got some e-mails to answer. Rock on.

Diagnosing Red Eyes

Red eye and other symptoms can be the amateur doctor's toughest diagnosis, and a challenge that tempts cubicle inhabitants across the nation into breaching the unwritten *Don't ask, don't tell* corporate policy regarding obvious ailments, injuries, and conspicuous wounds. If the individual with the red eyes displays a behavior that could be considered overtly neurotic, suicidal, shocked, depressed, or grief-stricken, the polite and nonconfrontational question that should be asked is the classic, "Are you all right?" This demonstrates that the question asker is a decent person who acknowledges being in the presence of suffering and cares about the person who is in pain, yet also respects the sufferer enough not to pry into their personal business. The power shift now lies with the red-eyed individual; the burden of giving or repressing information is his or hers, and your colleague can decide when, if, and how the details are made public.

Managing the Cubicle Hypochondriac

In every collection of people there is a dog lover, a cat hater, a failed vegetarian, an alcoholic, a health nut, an egomaniac, an insecure pale person, an overweight football fan—and a hypochondriac. Workplace hypochondriacs turn their cubicles into virtual pharmacies of over-the-counter and prescription medications. They are constantly afflicted by the weather they are never out in. In spring the pollen gives them terrible allergies. In summer they are dehydrated and suffer from mysterious bug bites. In fall they always feel something "coming on," which everyone knows is the hypochondriac's favorite season: winter. During the winter months they always feel "flu-ish" and sneeze regularly just to prove it. Sometime between Thanksgiving and Christmas they stock their cubicle with various nose sprays, nondrowsy medicines, and pills of all shapes, colors, and sizes. One thing hypochondriacs are not afraid of is talking. And they especially love to talk about their area of expertise—diseases, particularly the ones they don't really have. In truth, hypochondriacs do suffer from a disease— hypochondria. So they should be treated with a level of sympathy and respect that does not entirely indulge their need for gratification and further medical conjecture. The line between being caring and dismissive can be a tough one to walk. Take the following situation.

Katie Jones is a twenty-two-year-old student who recently graduated from Bennington College in Vermont. After she moved back in with her parents, her father explained to her, "My house, my rules." Katie had to get a job immediately, even if it wasn't in her academic major, Suburban Theories of the 1980s. Though she did learn how to play the keyboard and sew her own shoulder pads into her wardrobe, Katie's skill set was not landing her any jobs in the current economy. So, like young people in the old days, Katie took a job that she didn't want at goliath Cubers International, and she didn't complain about the money, the people, or the advancement opportunities. Katie's parents taught her the value of an honest day's work, and she appreciated talking to the older employees about "what it was like back then." This gave Katie a great sense of gratification. She was gaining firsthand knowledge of a time period that she barely remembered. And she was able to confirm the validity of her forty-page senior thesis, "The Dawn of AIDS: Modern Techniques for Stereotyping Tragedy." Which brings us to something Katie didn't expect: Eric Shuman, a perpetually woozy midlevel graphic designer. And a hypochondriac.

Adventures in Hypochondria
Cubers International Receptionist's Desk, Twenty-second Floor. 11:49 AM.

Eric: I thought I had AIDS for about six years.
Katie: Really? That's horrible.
Eric: Back then people thought you could get AIDS from kissing, and, well, my grandmother kissed me

at a Christmas party in 1989, rocketing me into the at-risk group.

Katie: Gosh!

Eric: About that same time I got some rare form of pneumonia that the doctors can't even identify. I have good days and bad days, but it won't ever go away completely. *Cough. Cough.*

Katie: You should really take better care of yourself. Do you take vitamins?

Eric: No, vitamins make my urine glow. But the big guy let me put a humidifier in my cubicle to free up my breathing. I keep it in the corner so it doesn't make my clothes damp and give me a cold.

Katie: Well, that's nice.

Eric: It is, but it doesn't help with germs. Germs love moisture. I have to leave the kitchen when I see people using that same sponge one after another. Did you know a dry sponge has fewer germs than a wet sponge soaked in dishwashing liquid?

Katie: No, I didn't. Thank God we have health insurance!

Eric: I don't have health insurance. I work on a contract basis.

Katie: What? Aren't you afraid of getting hit by a bus?

Eric: No offense, Katie, but you sound paranoid. You need to relax.

Quick Quiz Self-Assessment

(1) Fill in the blanks:

Work: Hey, Tom, I heard you called in sick today. How are you?

Tom: I've been better. You know how it is with things like this, you've just got to let them run their course.

Work: I hear you. Listen, I hate to . . .

Tom: _____.

Work: As I was saying, I hate to bother you while you're sick at home, but do you know where the general proposal form is saved on the shared drive?

Tom: It's on the Z drive in the "projects" folder in the "proposal" subfolder.

Work: Thanks. Again, I'm sorry to bother you while you're sick.

Tom: _____. No problem. _____.

    (a) You are being rude.

        I don't believe you, but anyway.

        You've always been an inconsiderate ass.

    (b) *Cough.*

        Cough.

        Cough.

    (c) Grandma? Is that you? Are you driving a Big Wheel? I'm sorry. Go ahead.

        There's a three-legged dog yelping in my closet.

        Wait. Now it's a shoe rack again.

(2) True or False? Several websites that specialize in office furniture now sell customized cubicle versions of the Plexiglas sneeze guards found at chain restaurant salad bars. As visitors cross an ankle-level security beam, the lightweight sneeze guard is lowered from shiny chains attached to light fixtures above, comfortably enveloping the visitor with a four-by-four-foot pyramid-shaped Plexiglas shield. These revolutionary sneeze guards are available in three colors: classic clear, mint green, and champagne yellow, and retail for ninety-five dollars.

(3) A young female colleague stumbles out of the bathroom clutching a dozen withered roses. Her eyes are red. Her nose is running. She coughs four times and then vomits on the carpet. She smells like cheap booze. What is she suffering from?

    (a) A cold.

    (b) The flu.

    (c) A broken heart, followed by a drinking binge that weakened her immune system to the point at which she caught a cold, then the flu, all before her hangover kicks in.

    (d) A migraine.

ANSWERS:

(1) b. (2) False. Politically correct corporate environments do not allow cubicle dwellers to defend themselves against sick colleagues. (3) c.

CHAPTER FIVE

Eating, Drinking, and Digesting

Aromas, Odors, and the Smell of Success

On the cubicle farm, nothing furrows eyebrows, wrinkles noses, or twists faces more than food that stinks. In a stale and colorless environment such as the workplace, smells take on added dimensions. They are more defined, ambulant, and ghostly. Chicken à la king becomes a poltergeist that haunts the accounting department. The smell of microwaved meat loaf follows a passing receptionist from the kitchen into the hallway like a lonely apparition longing for companionship. The musty scent of blue cheese levitates from a chef's salad in cubicle D-14 to spread through surrounding cubicles like a fog in a graveyard. Smells, like ghosts, are creepy. You can't see them, but you know they are with you, if not in you, haunting your nasal cavities and esophageal passages like a moaning vapor from a Scooby-Doo cartoon. So remember, in the hauntingly cartoonish environment of the cubicle farm, no one wants to be possessed by your vegetarian ravioli.

Although your colleagues understand your need to eat at

your cubicle, they don't appreciate smelling food that makes them hungry, irritated, or nauseous. Being considerate of those around you is an essential characteristic of being professional. Just as you don't hang distasteful pictures in your cubicle or make offensive comments to your colleagues, it is equally important not to bother your co-workers with objectionable smells. Enjoying your self-constructed London broil burrito while not causing your neighbors to salivate onto their keyboards is a difficult balancing act. The issue of food smells in the workplace is a quintessential example of the problems that can arise when the rights of the individual clash with the rights of the

community. Sure, smoking is no longer permitted in workplaces because lifestyles finally caught up with scientific evidence, but how strenuously, if at all, should we regulate annoyances on the cubicle farm? When are an individual's rights to eat smelly food infringed upon, or even overturned, for the sake of the greater corporate society? Patrick Finnegan is two weeks behind schedule and needs to work through lunch in order to process his invoices on time. Is it acceptable that his love of sardines and onion dip distracts Sally Silverstone from doing her job efficiently? Does Patrick's lunch become a moral issue because it influences Sally Silverstone's productivity and assaults her own rights to a comfortable and pleasant-smelling work area? We'll answer these questions and more in the following pages.

First, we need to understand the smelling process. Why do we need smell, and how does it work?

Your sense of smell is a chemical process developed to inform your brain about potential dangers such as spoiled eggs, approaching forest fires, cheaply perfumed mothers-in-law, gasoline leaks, and pungent grizzly bears that stalk campsites. Smell requires that tiny molecules float through the air into your nostrils, and onto neurons that act like taste buds—except these neurons specialize in aromas instead of flavors. That is why steaming leftover ravioli smells and your mouse pad does not (if it does, get a new one immediately). Of course, our sense of smell does more than warn us about danger; it also alerts us to things that are appealing, fresh, sexy, and clean. Old Spice, hippies selling incense, Gucci, raspberry-scented candles, green mouthwash, drug-addled models, Mennen, cardboard pine trees that hang from rearview mirrors, cologne, and fabric softeners have all garnered fortunes from attractive scents. Smell is a very powerful human sense with deep connections to memories and emotions. Assaults to this sense in a professional environment have never been directly addressed by the regulations of corporate political correctness. It is difficult to tell people that the food they enjoy smells like interstate roadkill, particularly if the meal has a link to cultural heritage, emotional history, or religious doctrine.

As a rule, if you are over the age of eighteen and encounter a dish that you have never heard of and can't pronounce, withhold all personal comments. Following up your own ignorance with an opinion is behaving like those idiots who wander into the middle of rush hour and then start directing traffic so they don't get killed. So, within reason, be thoughtful of what other people eat and how it smells. Unless you write for *Gourmet* magazine and regularly describe your food as being "gastronomically sub-Saharan, yet flippant" or "autumnal but precocious," keep your drive-thru-breakfast-and-frozen-dinner upbringing to yourself. There is no shame in knowing how to doctor up a frozen pizza. But don't condescend to less informed colleagues who think *Stouffer's, Marie Callender's, Hot Pockets,* and *Lean Cuisine* are hip street names for narcotics that you heat on a spoon.

SAMPLE CONVERSATIONS

Poor Choice of Language
Office Kitchen. 12:22 PM.

Chad: Hey, Maharishna. You're not the only one who needs to microwave their lunch.

Megawati: My name is Megawati. And it's only fifty-two more seconds.

Chad: That's cool. I'll just call you Taj, like in Taj Mahal? Is that cool? I'm not good with Indian names.

Megawati: I'm not Indian. I'm Indonesian.

Chad: Relax, Taj. I'm not criticizing you. We don't have the caste system in America.

Microwave: Ding!

Megawati (removing lunch): The microwave is yours.

Chad: What's that smell?

Megawati: It's *ajam djahe mangga majeera.* Stir-fried chicken with ginger and mango.

Chad: Well, it smells like a dead cat with ginger and mango. Someone call the ASPCA! Taj Mahal over here is heating up Garfield for lunch.

Megawati: My mother made it for me as a child. I eat it every year for lunch on the anniversary of her death.

Chad: Taj, you ever think it was eating cat that killed your mom in the first place? You're in a caste where you have to eat cat to survive! Whoa. No wonder you came to America.

Excellent Choice of Language
Office Kitchen. 12:22 PM.

Chad: Hi. I'm Chad. Do you mind if I use the microwave after you?

Megawati: Sure. My name is Megawati. And it's only fifty-two more seconds.

Chad: Thanks.

Microwave: Ding!

Megawati (removing lunch): The microwave is yours.

Chad: What's that smell?

Megawati: It's *ajam djahe mangga majeera.* Stir-fried chicken with ginger and mango.

Chad: I can't say that appeals to me. But then again, I don't have a real appreciation for ethnic food.

Megawati: My mother made it for me as a child. I eat it every year for lunch on the anniversary of her death.

Chad: That's great. My mother doesn't really cook. Except for that time she lit my stepdad's Camaro on fire. Our cat was in the backseat.

The reality of cubicle life is different from the video that human resources made you watch on orientation day. The smells you bring to the cubicle farm are as important to your reputation as anything you may do, wear, or say. There are far more smells on the cubicle farm than there are people; these scents, and their combinations, create an infinite number of odorous possibilities ranging from enchanting to rancid. Yet because smells are so difficult to regulate and contain, they are perhaps the most complained-about infraction of cubicle etiquette.

For example, Brad Laudenbaumer wore a three-hundred-dollar pair of leather shoes and a dashing blue-and-yellow-checkered tie on his first day of work at Cubers International, Inc. The stick deodorant he applied to his armpits that morning canceled out any signs of nervousness. Even his new photo ID card was too blurred to reveal the dark tooth that plagued his smile. Incredibly, Sharona, the hot receptionist, reciprocated a seemingly sincere interest in his hobby of collecting old circus programs. After shaking hands with his boss's boss, Brad Laudenbaumer went to lunch. He returned with garlic shrimp from Lucky Hope Key takeout, which he ate in his new cubicle, transforming the entire marketing department into a Chinatown back alley. It wasn't until three months later, at the office holiday party, that a drunk colleague grabbed his arm and said, "Heeey, do you know why everyone calls you Jackie Chan?"

The Toaster Oven

Toaster ovens are susceptible to abuse because they provide employees with the toasting or grilling option. In an environment where people feel as if they are denied the good things in life, they will fully exploit any opportunity to engage in luxury. Even if that means toasting celery sticks. Though allowing toaster-oven use is a noble attempt by the corporation to reach out to employees, it also encourages unproductive and self-indulgent behavior. The toaster oven creates a traffic jam of people waiting to burn their peanut butter sandwiches and grill lunch meats piled on crackers under those glowing orange coils. The toaster oven is the duct tape of kitchen appliances: It can fix any culinary problem. Toaster-oven abuse begins with breakfast as people toast bagels and piece together makeshift egg-and-cheese breakfast sandwiches. After all, when you are at work, you are officially clocked in. For many employees, after they log in, it's breakfast time.

The Microwave Oven

The microwave oven was invented in 1946 by Dr. Percy Spencer, a self-taught engineer. While employed by the Raytheon Corporation, Dr. Spencer noticed that a candy bar had melted in his pocket while he was working on an experimental vacuum tube called a magnetron. In 1975, for the first time since the Manhattan Project, Americans bought more microwave ovens than gas ranges. Soon after this technological landmark every helpless bachelor, incompetent housewife, latchkey child, retired husband, bungling teenager, and hapless cubicle denizen instantly became a third-rate chef. Frozen black bean quiches, plastic dishes of diet linguini in clam sauce, Salisbury steaks beneath punctured cellophane wrappers, microwavable bowls

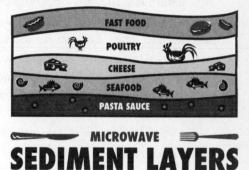

of soup, and five-day-old pepperoni pizza replaced Wonder Bread bologna sandwiches and plastic-wrapped peanut butter and crackers. As a result, the American workplace would never be the same. The smells of gourmet crap food replaced the nonsmells of regular crap food. To this day the regulations of corporate human resource departments have not caught up with the lightning speed of microwave technology invented in 1946. Until now, there has only been an unspoken and unconfirmed set of parameters regarding the effect microwaved food, and its smell, has on one's professional reputation.

For decades now both independent and government-sponsored health programs have spouted the catchy phrase *You are what you eat* to encourage Americans to be healthier. It is true: The food you put into your body affects how you look, feel, and behave. This useful maxim also rings true on the cubicle farm. The health of your reputation—how you are perceived by your colleagues—is greatly influenced by your dining habits. Not only does your food choice determine how much you weigh, how much energy you have, and whether or not you need to take a multivitamin, but it also says more than you may think about your values and station in life.

Like a mud pool in the African desert, the office microwave attracts every species of employee during lunch hour. Like rhinos, flamingos, and antelope, employees from far-flung departments cautiously approach one another before deciding to intermingle. They awkwardly assess one another. They compare lives. They compare appearances. They compare lunches.

For some inexplicable reason many cubicle dwellers think the *You are what you eat* rule only applies to others. Take the following scenarios.

Tammy Rothchild is an outwardly beautiful and secure twenty-five-year-old who claims to eat "whenever and whatever I want." Yet Tammy's colleagues have never seen her eat anything other than carrot sticks. They would not be surprised to hear that Tammy never eats breakfast and cries in the shower before going to bed every night. Tammy is not just on a diet; she is on a hunger strike for her father's love, a father whom she has not seen in twelve years. Yet as Tammy's colleagues stand around the microwave and stare at their squares of Tupperware and containers of microwavable soup, they do not comment when she passes by with her ziplock of carrot sticks. Tammy's colleagues know better than to gossip about her during lunch break in front of the microwave. That is what stairwells and smoke breaks are for. Besides, they are busy living their own lies.

Mrs. Hamdinger does not realize that her condescending attitude and oversize diamond wedding ring with the band of "Blue Canyon" sapphire gemstones doesn't fool any of her colleagues. The same plump ring finger that flashes around a four-carat rock also gets burned every afternoon when removing overheated Stouffer's Fettuccini Alfredo from a microwave encrusted with six-month-old Chinese food. Mrs. Hamdinger's colleagues know why she doesn't have a personal chef or eat lunch at Melito's Gourmet: She lives on a tight budget, just like they do. The rich and pretentious may be able to justify their entitled lifestyles on *Access Hollywood,* MTV, star-studded award ceremonies, and so-called reality shows, but in the cubicle community you either live your life as it is or you live a lie everyone can see through.

Samuel McCallister hangs his framed diploma from Dartmouth College (bachelor of arts in Middle English literature) in his cubicle and eats Hot Pockets for lunch four times a week. He takes himself out for pizza every Friday, where he sits alone and fills up on the buffet and free refills. He knows everything about Dartmouth. The history. The campus. The required SAT scores for admission. Samuel McCallister graduated from Dartmouth nine years ago. Samuel believes that graduating from an Ivy League school makes him not only better than other people, but also happier than other people. For example, when Tara Vasquez, an immigrant from Peru who recently finished her A-plus certification at the local community college, fixes Samuel's problems networking to the shared printer, he says, "Thanks, Tara. At Dartmouth we don't take classes that teach you how to fix a flat tire or set up a printer. We study complex concepts like 'Urban Western Identity in the 1800s' and 'The Role of Gender in Revolutions.' Maybe if your kids study hard, one of them will go to Dartmouth someday. Ivy League schools really open a lot of doors that would otherwise be shut. I may be able to pull some strings."

The only string that Samuel McCallister pulls is the one that winds onto the cardboard circle on the back of the Interdepartment Delivery envelope (the kind with the holes in it so you know when it's empty), which he has to walk over to processing by 3 PM every afternoon.

Insecure cubicle inhabitants promote an image instead of a soul. Sadly, oftentimes they end up getting fired or disciplined because of their lies and inaccurate characterizations of themselves. Young and beautiful Tammy Rothchild said she couldn't eat cake at her boss's birthday party because there wasn't enough for everyone and she wanted to be polite. When Bob from promotions handed her an extra piece, Tammy melted down, throwing the cake and the napkin it was on across the room, where it struck and briefly stuck to a window. With bloodshot eyes she shouted, "You think your damn cake is going to teach me about love!"

When Mrs. Hamdinger's husband left her for Charles Perry, the Newington Country Club's new head chef, she microwaved her wedding ring on HIGH and set fire to the Chinese-food-splattered interior. It wasn't until 4:15 PM that afternoon that the fire department allowed employees back in the building.

Ivy Leaguer Samuel McCallister broke into tears and started spouting racial slurs against Latinos after the new marketing analyst, Kate Garcia, a Harvard graduate with a double major in Middle Eastern poetry and Japanese language (with a minor in Inu mythology), was hired. She and Tara Vasquez refused to speak English around Samuel, which made him feel stupid, inferior, sad, and angry. The caricatures he drew of them on the bathroom stall were not well received by his colleagues. When Samuel returned from his mandatory vacation two weeks later, he had difficulty explaining how someone could spend two

Eating, Drinking, and Digesting

```
S G H L E F T O V E R S M F O S S X T R O M
P Y M N D A M V X D F F O P Y U S E V I Z Q
U A R O M A A K C E T R K C O Y F H S G Y G
I O S S C S L H G U I B S O H F T A S T E Y
K N V M U T N H V X E Z J N Q R Y I V K Z B
H I S M Z E G S D O L M E Q S X D E T G K T
H Y V B D Y L D U J V F N X D C F V J I P X
E B U I J K S A L A D I E S F E Z E P O D C
I R C N X Q A P O T C C P O P C O R N M P R
S J I E S S V N G F Q P L Y O K P V U U R F
M F C V G Y U H I D E W D F W U I F P H B U
E F G H U Y T B V A S W P H U I N C D X Y W
L K H M M I C R O W A V E N B V R S G H J O
L V X Y G G H R W A I O C U B E R S I N T L
```

AROMA		TASTE		YUM	
SMELL		MICROWAVE		LEFTOVERS	
CUBERS INTL		SALAD		POPCORN	

weeks at a tropical resort in the Caribbean and not have any hint of a tan. Rumors spread that he'd had a nervous breakdown. To prove a point, Samuel tacked a postcard of a tropical Caribbean sunset onto his cubicle wall. To prove a point, Tara Vasquez bought the same postcard at the Zip Mart down the street and hung it in her cubicle, too.

People who work in cubicles are generally intelligent, educated, and perceptive. They have goals, are ambitious, and want to succeed. They understand that we live in a superficial society and people are often measured by things other than the quality of their hearts, the speed of their minds, or the integrity of their character. What car you drive to work says a lot about you. So do the clothes you wear to work. So does what you eat for lunch at work. Of course, the most together and self-confident cubicle dwellers know that the opinions of other people are insignificant. For the rest of us, however, here is a primer on what our food is saying about us.

TUPPERWARE: *I'm on a budget.*

If you microwave your lunch in a Tupperware container, you are budgeting. Even if your meal is sliced Pacific salmon topped with beluga caviar on imported Italian bread, you're being economical. Anyone who would microwave salmon, caviar, and bread obviously attended a wedding reception the previous weekend where someone they knew married up in status. Yet do not despair over Tupperware. These plastic containers and their snappy lids are an American tradition. Being economical and financially savvy is a tribute to Depression-era grandfathers and great-grandmothers everywhere. Furthermore, Tupperware is for cubicle dwellers who have other people in their lives. Eating leftovers means eating a meal that was probably designed for more than one. Lonely people don't cook for groups and don't microwave leftovers with more than one food group. Moms microwave leftover basil chicken breast with peas and carrots. Bachelors microwave leftover pizza, and they usually do that in unraveled Saran Wrap or some form of flimsy plate. Everyone knows those pizza-shaped Tupperware containers don't really accommodate real pizza slices, no matter how many rubber bands you wrap around them.

FROZEN DIET FOOD: *I am a woman.* Or *I am a fifty-two-year-old heart attack candidate on strict orders from my doctor.* Or *I am a gay man.*

Women, health-conscious fifty-somethings, and gay men use their heads when it comes to weight loss. They calculate calories, measure their body dimensions, and actually think about body fat proportions relative to height and age. Unsupervised straight men bullishly exercise their way to weight loss, often converting time on the treadmill to numbers of Sam Adams and dumbbell reps to future roast beef sandwiches; they wouldn't voluntarily eat a Lean Cuisine Chicken Portabello or Jenny Craig Turkey with Gravy even if it were free. Diet meals in the microwave imply to your colleagues, *I have goals and I'm working to either reduce my weight or maintain it.* It's an act of discipline and a form of lunch widely respected by cubicle dwellers, even if the diet isn't working. America's fight against obesity begins with an effort, and frozen diet meals in the office microwave are indicative of cubicle dwellers fighting not just obesity, but also the oppressive and sedentary corporate environment that requires them to sit down all day.

ORIGINAL BOXES AND CONTAINERS: *I'm selfish, inconsiderate, and lazy.*

Don't bring your two leftover pieces of Romano's sausage-and-onion pizza to work in the box they were delivered in. There is a restricted amount of space in the company refrigerator. In a way, the corporate refrigerator is a great social experiment that tests employees' ability to respect and consider the needs of their peers with limited supervision. Just as cubicles are designed to provide humans barely enough work space to remain sane, corporate refrigerators are designed to provide lunches barely enough shelf space to remain cool. So be thoughtful. Those three bites of Oreo cheesecake don't belong in that large rectangular plastic container from The Cheesecake Factory. You are forcing your colleagues to cram their sandwiches into the butter bin on the door or into the crisper drawers. Congratulations on your discipline, but your date isn't going to think you are a pig if you finish your desert. If you just can't eat another bite, leave it behind, take it home and eat it later, or—if you must bring it to work—put it in a smaller, less space-consuming container.

Supermarket salad bars have forever changed the way Americans eat salad. They have also forever changed the way Americans eat leftover salad. In our self-conscious and cleverly self-deceptive minds, Americans quickly made the connection that because salads are healthy, we can put together a wholesome thirty-nine-pound salad for lunch. Throw on the mini corn cobs, ham squares the size of Rubik's Cubes, boiled eggs, crunchy bacon bits, cinder blocks of cheddar cheese, chemically fertilized tomato slices, and croutons that look like foam dice, and we still believe we're eating better than Richard Simmons. As long as it has lettuce in it, it's a healthy salad. As long as we can't finish it, we're really cutting back on calories. Since we can't finish it, we take it to work the following morning. Salads, after all, go bad after a couple of days. After the dawn of the supermarket salad bar, corporate refrigerators everywhere were soon filled with oversized, clear plastic containers full of wilted iceberg lettuce drowning in oil and balsamic vinegar, mushroom stems smothered in day-old ranch dressing, and soggy onions mired in blue cheese and bean sprouts. Salads take up little space, particularly the day after they are made. So don't bring original salad containers to work. They are not space-friendly and often unexpectedly flip open like Vietcong booby traps. Transfer your leftover salad into something smaller—a Tupperware container, Saran-Wrapped cereal bowl, or even ziplock bag. Anything to save space and show you care about the cubicle community.

THE BULK APPROACH: *Since the mission statement says I'm part of our corporate family, I'm making myself at home.*

Most cubicle dwellers understand that part of adapting to corporate culture means curtailing their personal lives. Employees purposefully stifle their private personalities, opinions, and quirks while at the office. Mark Lazar doesn't want his colleagues to know that his favorite hobby is needlepoint. Beth Weatherford never mentions that she can't stand it when her colleagues chew gum—it makes them look like dirty cattle—and, in fact, she has never had a piece of gum in her life. Vivian Momack's favorite color is bright red, but she always wears brown pants and gray shirts because she doesn't want people to notice her, especially her boss. The corporate environment is designed to make everyone anonymous and small. It is the reality of cubicle life.

Accordingly, the corporate refrigerator is designed for small meals, similar to those they serve on airplanes or that contestants eat on *Survivor*. Neither the office refrigerator nor the kitchen was intended for family-size jars of grape jelly, Costco plastic barrels of pretzels, a leftover turkey carcass Saran Wrapped to a cookie sheet, or sprawling sandwich assembly lines of meats, bread slices, vegetables, and cheeses. Any meal that requires kitchen appliances or cookbooks should be carefully scrutinized. Though many office kitchens allow employees use of a toaster oven, some misguided cubicle dwellers exploit this appliance as if it were the gas grill they use to cook hot dogs, corn on the cob, and hamburgers at their Fourth of July party. The office toaster oven is for melting cheese on a bagel, not for cooking a western omelet in an aluminum dish you stole from your niece's Betty Crocker lightbulb oven. Cubicle dwellers are optimistic people by nature, but there is a difference between taking lemons and making lemonade and taking a toaster oven and making a crabmeat-and-asparagus soufflé. One means you are practical. The other means you are a jerk.

Recently hired employees understand the importance of being accepted by their colleagues. They need to fit in professionally and socially. They don't bring complicated meals to the workplace. They don't solicit unwanted attention or invite controversy. Veteran cubicle people, however, are different. They're cocky. They fart in the bathroom like they own the place. They're disrespectful. They borrow the stapler, HTML book, and box of tissues from your cube and never return any of it. They're condescending. They glide over to the printer and cancel your print job so theirs goes to the head of the queue. "Sorry, but this is important," they explain.

Yet eventually, many veteran bureaucrats fall prey to their false sense of comfort. Over the years the lack of sensitivity evolves into a complete abandonment of common sense.

Veteran employees, for instance, kick back in their cubes like they do in their living rooms.

Or they flirt with and confide in colleagues, setting the stage for a "work husband" or "work wife" where emotional cheating can lead to strained relations with the "real husband" or "real wife."

Or they fill the office refrigerator with a dozen eggs, a twenty-four-ounce squeeze bottle of mustard, and an entire gallon of milk. They stock the cupboards with a two-pound jar of olives, a loaf of bread, two liters of Diet Pepsi, and restaurant-size spice containers of oregano, thyme, basil, and coriander. They think they are at home and that co-workers are guests who invited themselves over.

Power Struggles in the Kitchen

Unfortunately, the kitchen creates an environment where alpha males and alpha females attempt to enforce their seniority and sense of entitlement.

For example, eight years ago when Michael Sherman became an assistant web producer at Cubers International, he ate lunch by himself every day at his cubicle. Michael was shy, owned two pairs of pleated khakis, which he wore alternately, and was terrified of small talk. Whenever anyone in the kitchen spoke to him, Michael would panic and stammer out words incoherently, as if engaged in a conversation while urinating on the third rail of a city subway. "Hey, Michael. How are you?" a colleague would ask. "I'm good—okay. Fine. I. Okay. I mean. You fine. Or good?" He would then swing open the refrigerator door, yank out his brown-bag lunch—peanut butter sandwich and a bag of Wise potato chips—and scamper back to the security of his cubicle like a cat with a chipmunk in its mouth. After settling in and regrouping, he would return to the kitchen and anxiously feed coins into the soda machine for his Diet Coke.

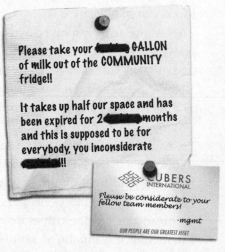

Now, at age thirty-two, Michael Sherman has the experience and confidence that have caused countless midlevel bureaucrats to behave like idiots. Two years ago he cheated on his wife with Annie Dunn, a marketing analyst who has since relocated to Riverside, California. Michael then bought a Porsche and wrecked it coming home from a poker game. During the dot-com bubble of the late 1990s Michael was even relocated into an office and given a secretary. Two weeks later his secretary quit and was never replaced. Shortly after that Michael was moved out of his office and back into a cubicle so the office could be used as a "safe place" to store computers during a companywide restructuring. To this day the office remains locked and full of old IBM desktops. No one knows who has the key. Nevertheless, during his progression as a Cubers International employee and as a man, Michael's culinary acumen evolved dramatically. He read in a popular men's magazine that for men in their thirties, sex drive and performance are greatly influenced by diet. A survey of one hundred anonymous women revealed that 80 percent claimed sex was "more satisfying" after their significant others switched to an all-organic diet. Furthermore, these same women were "three times more likely to reciprocate sexual satisfaction" upon experiencing orgasm as opposed to providing pleasure to their lovers out of obligation.

Nothing fed or sprayed with chemicals entered Michael's body again. He became an enthusiastic organic-food advocate and meticulous eater. When he shopped at The Green Leaf and Organic Beef Gourmet Food Boutique he stocked up on nature as if he were preparing for a famine in a postapocalyptic world run by preservative executives. Michael unwaveringly eats Pennsylvania goat cheese and imported Northern Italian prosciutto on toasted French bread slices drizzled with extra-virgin olive oil. And he only drinks soy milk from Wisconsin. Every Monday, Michael places his purchases in what he tells himself is "his section" of the corporate refrigerator. While cutting and assembling the untainted sandwiches on the limited counter space, Michael dirties four plates (which he washed thoroughly after grabbing them from the communal cupboard), two plastic forks, and two plastic knives, which he leaves behind in the sink when he leaves. Over the years he's learned to ignore the notecard taped below the cabinets that reads "Please Clean Up After Yourselves and Keep the Kitchen Area Neat! Thank You for Your Cooperation. —Corporate Services and Your Colleagues." Unfortunately for Michael, his sense of entitlement and dues paid to the company is about to be challenged by Martha Wynn, corporate services head administrator at Cubers International. They meet each other as he is clearing a space in the refrigerator for the gallon of soy milk he bought because his previous gallon is set to expire in three days.

Sample Kitchen Power Struggle
Office Refrigerator. 1:11 PM.

Martha: Michael, do you realize what a mess you're leaving behind? The bread crumbs? The dishes in the sink? The plastic forks and knives that could be easily discarded in the trash?

Michael: It's the kitchen. What do you expect? If this were the conference room, you might have a point.

Martha: Don't you think it's disrespectful to your colleagues, not to mention the cleaning staff?

Michael: The cleaning people get paid to clean up the kitchen. Are you saying I should put them out of a job? Hey, we all gotta start somewhere. Welcome to capitalism. Should I go clean the toilets, too, because I took a crap there this morning?

Martha: Ugh. You're impossible. You act like you own everything—the kitchen, the refrigerator.

Michael: Well, I don't own the kitchen and I don't own the refrigerator, but I do own the soy milk you see. And the imported prosciutto. And the nine-dollar-a-pound goat cheese. It's not my fault you don't get here early enough to claim your own space in the refrigerator.

Martha: But you aren't entitled to all the space your food takes up. On the kitchen counter or in the refrigerator.

Michael: Says who? I don't own the parking spaces, either, but if I get here early enough, I know I can park on level one in the garage. I get up early and get to work early. Don't blame me for parking or taking up refrigerator space just because you can't get out of bed in the morning.

Martha: Fine. Just forget it.

Michael: Fine. Already forgotten. You ever think about going on a diet? You could drop twenty pounds by going organic. Just smell this goat cheese.

Rules for the Kitchen

In the world of capitalism, time is money. And now more than ever, so is space. There is a war of attrition between corporate overhead and employee comfort. Don't be fooled: The company always wins. But that doesn't mean cubicle dwellers are helpless in the kitchen. By being considerate of one another's gastronomical needs, cubicle residents can create a community where respect for others and basic humanity temper the imposing presence of the corporate bottom line. Below are rules that all office kitchens require for the needs of the community to succeed over the wants of individual employees.

RULE 1: COVER YOUR FOOD IN THE MICROWAVE

Leftover Chinese food, bowls of chicken soup, and last night's lasagna all spit and splatter in the office microwave. So cover them up. Paul Swanson over at cube K-47 in the finance department is an amateur geologist. He understands how loose particles settle on top of one another, become compressed into distinct layers, and create strata that can reveal the secrets of history and teach us about the past. Paul Swanson knows why everyone's lunch smells and tastes like moo goo gai pan. It's because Kristin Loring, who works at the front desk, didn't cover her food when she microwaved it. As a result, her leftover Chinese bubbled like lava before spewing streams of hot soy sauce and hurling grains of rice and bamboo shoots against the microwave walls, ceiling, and windowed door. From outside the microwave looking in, it appeared as if Chinese New Year had been hit by a car. Paul Swanson watched Kristin Loring quickly retrieve her meal from the microwave and disappear into the chaos of lunch hour. No one bothered to clean the microwave, and every burrito, pot roast, and Hot Pocket thereafter smelled of—as they say in the wine business—a "hint" of moo goo gai pan. Not only that, but because ensuing employees also refused to cover their food, every time an employee heated an uncovered meal in the microwave, he or she added another level of smell and food sediment to the growing landscape of lunches from the past. If it weren't for the cleaning staff or fed-up employees, in a million years or so these layers of gook would produce oil and diamonds.

Also, even if you can't see the food material being heated into a liquid and slung throughout the oven, it doesn't mean the tainting process isn't occurring. In microwaves heated food molecules are tossed around like millions of dirty socks in a nuclear-driven dryer. Sure, you can watch soup burp and vapor shoot from the corner of a bag of popcorn as if it were a broken steam pipe, but it's what you can't see that affects the taste and smell of your lunch. Molecules, though small, are powerful. Scary things become part of—meld into—your food. Why does your once delicious and satisfying red bean chili smell and taste like pepperoni pizza? What happened? Your red bean chili experienced the same fate as Jeff Goldblum in 1986's eerily microwavable horror film sensation *The Fly*. In the movie Jeff Goldblum's character, the brilliant but eccentric scientist Seth Brundle, transports himself from one transmission booth (big microwave) to another. In the process of being heated on high for five and a half minutes, something goes terribly wrong. His molecules become mixed with the molecules of a fly that chose a terrible place to enjoy all flies' favorite pastime—bumping into glass over and over again. By the time the microwaving process is over, the fly and Jeff have become one, which explains the hair. Anyway, let's say your red bean chili is Jeff Goldblum, and the pepperoni pizza residue that you never accounted for is the fly. Zap on high for three minutes, and you get a creepy combination of the two. The sequel, of course, is always worse.

RULE 2: IF YOU MAKE A MESS, CLEAN IT UP

This is what you teach your children. It's what your parents taught you. Cubicle inhabitants seem to forget their manners in the office kitchen. Rules can go too far, but we need them in order for society to function. So understand the negative effects your ignored spilled soda, leftover frozen-food box, or crusted tomato sauce in the microwave have on your professional society and personal reputation. Clean up after yourself. Don't act as if the office kitchen is your kitchen at home.

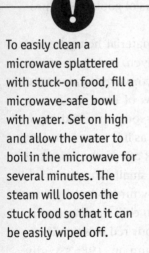

CUBE TIP

To easily clean a microwave splattered with stuck-on food, fill a microwave-safe bowl with water. Set on high and allow the water to boil in the microwave for several minutes. The steam will loosen the stuck food so that it can be easily wiped off.

RULE 3: DON'T STARE AT YOUR FOOD THROUGH THE MICROWAVE WINDOW

Get out of the way, even if you have to stir it. This rule addresses both obvious and veiled matters. First, microwaves are often located in high-traffic areas of the kitchen, especially during lunchtime. Standing in front of the microwave and staring at your food will not make it cook any quicker (as the saying goes, *A watched pot never boils*), and it makes you look like the kind of imbecile who laughs at insects having sex and writes letters to the weatherman on television requesting sunshine. Second, staring at invisible heat and an inanimate, turning chicken potpie can appear to your colleagues as an attempt to avoid eye contact and conversation. Even if your chicken potpie has more personality than your colleague, it is wise to act as though you care about your colleagues and willingly embark on conversations whenever given the opportunity. Remember that the kitchen is a social place; a distant countenance or antisocial behavior will be noticed, registered, and discussed by your colleagues. Nevertheless, when your meal is done, get out of the way of the microwave. People need it. Don't block access by adding salt, oregano, or other condiments to your food near the microwave. But before you leave the kitchen, make sure you haven't left a mess behind. Your colleagues will most definitely notice that, too.

RULE 4: CLOSE THE DOOR

The company refrigerator must be kept at forty degrees or cooler in order to slow the growth of bacteria. By leaving the refrigerator door ajar or continuously opening and closing it, you are allowing cold air to escape and are therefore jeopardizing not just your own food supply but also that of your cubicle community. As a precaution, refrigerated leftovers should be eaten in a day or two and not left too exposed to the unpredictable climate of the office refrigerator.

RULE 5: PROPERLY LABEL YOUR FOOD AND BE ACCOUNTABLE FOR IT

If you don't want your food stolen or thrown away, then make it known that it has an owner. Use a thick nonerasable pen (but not the type with the ink that stinks). Be clear. Don't use small, unmarked bottles (especially pill bottles) to import your favorite salad dressing or condiment from home. Don't rely on the goodness of human nature to protect your box of ice cream sandwiches in the freezer. They will disappear and in your misplaced frustration you may blame the wrong individual(s), setting yourself up for a Shakespearean-style fall from grace.

RULE 6: THE REFRIGERATOR IS FOR FOOD

Do not use the crisper to keep your nightcrawlers fresh for your fishing trip next weekend. Unless cleared with human resources, don't use the refrigerator to keep your medication cool, and don't store your alopecia prescription on the door between the ketchup and jar of olives. People will talk. Though it is politically incorrect, colleagues may have a problem with multiple packages of breast milk being left in the freezer next to the pint of mint chocolate chip ice cream and the abandoned bag of frozen corn.

RULE 7: REMEMBER JUDGMENT DAY

Many religious zealots have predicted the end of the world only to wake up to an awkward morning of chirping birds and unanswered prayers. Cubicle residents, however, can count on the day when everything in the office refrigerator comes to an end. So prepare for the refrigerator apocalypse. It's not difficult; actually, corporate services will tape a piece of paper to the refrigerator informing the cubicle inhabitants exactly when the day is coming. Hint—it's usually a Friday. The sign will look something like this:

Please Remove All of Your Food from the Refrigerator by Next Friday Because We Will Clean the Refrigerator and Discard All Remaining Items. Thank You for Your Cooperation.

Pay attention. The people at corporate services are not trying to judge you or make your life difficult. They're trying to help you, in their own mysterious ways. You have been warned, so you have no right to weep at the injustice in our universe when your yogurt suddenly goes missing. It's too late for prayer. It's too late to complain. You have no one but yourself to blame for where your yogurt goes on Judgment Day.

After the Kitchen

Eating lunch at one's cubicle is like being a cop in a doughnut shop. People understand a professional's right to a quiet moment with coffee and a chocolate cruller, but certain circumstances require that an employee drop everything and get back to work. So when you encounter a situation that requires the help of a colleague who is eating lunch in his or her cubicle, start by appraising the situation.

For example, before Tony Griego taps Alexa Crenshaw on the shoulder to ask about the Gupman ad templates, he should assess the urgency of the situation.

Poor Choice of Lunchtime Language
Cubicle 14-G, Eighth Floor. 1:37 PM.

Tony: Hey, Alexa. Do you have time for a question?
Alexa: Well, I have a fork full of Caesar salad, feta cheese stuck to my chin, and a piece of black olive I can't seem to unwedge from my teeth.
Alexa: Great. Have you had time to look at the Gupman ad templates? The jogger's leg blocks out one of the dog's back legs, so it looks like the dog only has three legs. That's probably not a good thing in a shoe campaign.

Alexa (setting down her fork and picking up a napkin): Ugh. Well, I haven't had time to look at them but I can do it now if they're that anxious. Did they just call you?

Tony: Oh, no. I'm not supposed to get back to them until next Wednesday. I was just wondering if you've taken a look at it.

Alexa (setting down the crumpled napkin): No, I haven't had time. I can do it now if that would make you feel better.

Tony: Oh my gosh, no. I wouldn't want to interrupt your lunch.

Excellent Choice of Lunchtime Language
Cubicle 14-G, Eighth Floor. 1:37 PM.

Tony: Hey, Alexa. Do you have time for a question?

Andrea: Well, I have a fork full of Caesar salad, feta cheese stuck to my chin, and a piece of black olive I can't seem to unwedge from my teeth.

Tony: I'm sorry. I should have seen that you were busy. I'll come back later at a more convenient time.

Alexa (rolling her tongue along her teeth): Thank you.

Guide to Recommended and Unrecommended Cubicle Foods

RECOMMENDED

- **Bread** doesn't smell unless it's straight from the oven or make noise unless it's stale or toasted. Bread has sustained the human race for centuries, perhaps because it's so inoffensive, inexpensive, and easy to consume.

- **Old-School Cheese.** Cheese that was popular more than ten years ago is ideal fare for cubicle eating. American cheese is perfect for snacking because it has little smell, comes in easily devoured portions that don't require chewing noises, and doesn't sound like plastic even though it may taste like it. Also, that awful string cheese that people feed their children in public venues to keep them quiet is equally appropriate in the cubicle community. Feta cheese, blue cheese, goat cheese, or any other cheese that is a good match for drinking wine is unacceptable.

- **Some Sandwiches.** Most sandwiches are relatively quiet and odorless. Nevertheless, other foods do not qualify for "Recommended" status simply by sticking them between two pieces of bread. A potato-chip-and-liver sandwich is not acceptable cubicle fare; a ham-and-old-school-cheese sandwich, however, is fine.

- **Salads.** Most salads are acceptable cubicle food assuming the consumer does not eat like a farm animal. Salads are relatively inoffensive in terms of smell; however, they can be noisy. When eating salads, make sure not to overstuff your mouth and for the love of God keep your mouth closed when you chew. Also, salad dressings do have a splatter factor, so be sure to cover up all important documents and expensive clothing with protective napkins.

- **Cafeteria Food.** In general, cafeteria food is food that resembles meals people make at home, when trying a recipe for the first time. Understandably, most cafeteria-goers stick with lunch staples such as pizza and pasta, both of which are recommended cubicle foods. Sure, there are many different types of pastas and pizzas, and they do emit easily detectable smells, but not for long. Once pasta and pizza cool down and stop steaming, their offensiveness decreases significantly. And if co-workers are eating cafeteria food in their cubicles, chances are it isn't very hot. Yet the office elevator may smell like oregano for a good fifteen minutes.

- **Nothing Else.** Just about anything cubicle residents eat in their cubicles will either smell, make noise, or annoy the neighbors. Sorry.

NOT RECOMMENDED
Everything else, especially:
- **Eggs.** Egg salad, boiled eggs, deviled eggs, or any meal that includes yolks. Their smell more than compensates for their lack of noise.

- **Gum.** There is nothing natural about gum. Scientists were paid by large companies to create this non-biodegradable goo full of artificial flavors derived from unnatural chemicals. Gum gives off more odor than the oranges and watermelons it is supposed to imitate. Also, any food or snack that requires extended chewing is suspect. People who chew gum and blow bubbles, snap, or slap it in their mouths should be escorted out of the building by security and placed in a fifth-grade homeroom where a nun slaps their knuckles with a wooden ruler.

- **Fish.** The ocean is magical, but the beach has breezes for a reason. Mackerel, sardines, microwaved fish sticks, and tuna fish sandwiches are all malodorous and therefore inappropriate choices for cubicle dining.

- **Popcorn.** The classic annoyance. If you want the smell, sound, and taste of popcorn in the cubicle community, then you'd better bring the entire movie experience to your colleagues and have Hilary Swank and Ethan Hawke show up, too.

- **Hot Dogs, BBQ, and Fries.** People eat these things at baseball games for a reason.

- **Potato Chips and Nachos.** Eating chips or nachos sounds the same as raking leaves. Spare colleagues the resonance of neighborhood yard work in the cubicle neighborhood.

Quick Quiz Self-Assessment

(1) True or False? The first microwave oven was concocted in 1949 by amateur inventor Wilma Dellington Conway, who lived in Wakefield, Rhode Island. After her husband was killed in action in World War II, she found it increasingly difficult to raise her four young boys as a single mother while working nights as a lab assistant at the nearby University of Rhode Island. She knew there must be some way to reduce the amount of time she spent every day cooking for her family. After three years of experimenting with the latest vacuum cleaner advances and glow-in-the-dark technology, she discovered that a blueberry pie she was making one day actually cooked in her hands as she carried it to the oven.

(2) Complete the following office kitchen conversation.

Samantha (holding her leftover chef's salad wrapped in a plastic 7-Eleven bag): What are these aluminum foil packages in the refrigerator? They're taking up all of the space.

Newton (smiling and smoothing out his mustache): That'll be the twelve-point buck I shot last Sunday. Got him coming out of a hedge grove at sunrise. Smack dab in the neck. He kept turning around like he was surprised by something, squirting blood from behind his ear. So I shot him again, and he went down like my drunk uncle Jake in a dodgeball game.

Samantha (holding open the refrigerator door in disgust): Are you telling me those aluminum foil packages are a chopped-up deer?

Newton (pointing at the refrigerator's contents): No, I'm not saying that at all. On Sunday it was a deer. Now it's venison. I've got rump roast right here on the bottom shelf. The neck is ground up like hamburger meat over there next to someone's Hot Pockets. In the crisper you got your brisket. Then up there on the top shelf is your loin chops. The flank is shoved onto the shelf in the door right there.

Samantha: Not only is this disgusting, but don't you think it's inappropriate and selfish to use the entire company refrigerator for your own benefit? What about everyone else's food?

Newton: Naw, I'm not being selfish at all. This here food is for everyone. You, me, those cleaning people who can't speak English. Everyone. Venison is a delicacy. This is supposed to be a gift.

Samantha: Well, Newton. Most people who give gifts, give things that other people might want. We have vegetarians in this office. We have animal rights activists. We have people who not only don't consider venison a delicacy, but might actually consider it primitive and, well, rednecky.

Newton: Then those folks don't have to eat it. They can just move it out of the way.

Samantha: That's what I'm saying, Newton. There is no space. Your dead deer is taking up the entire refrigerator.

Newton: Well, I guess I could take out the hooves and the head.

Samantha: You brought the hooves and the head?

Newton: Yep, I figured we'd get a good laugh out of watching someone who thinks they're getting delicious brisket or something unwrap the foil and find a head. Or the hooves. Heh, heh.

Samantha: _____.

(3) A tendril of steam rises from your neighbor's cubicle. Within seconds the intense smell of Orville Redenbacher's Gourmet Popping Corn, Ultimate Butter, sweeps over your senses like a summer rain shower. You begin to salivate. You can hear your colleague gleefully crunching handfuls of the sumptuous, hot, and buttery popcorn. You now crave it. List the following options in order of appropriateness.

    (a) Comment to your cubicle neighbor about how delicious the popcorn smells, hoping he will offer you a handful.

    (b) Be direct and ask your cubicle neighbor for a handful.

    (c) Tell your cubicle neighbor that you find the smell distracting and ask him to eat it elsewhere.

    (d) Tell him you are on a diet and find the smell distracting. Ask him to eat it elsewhere.

(e) Fart in his direction to counter the olfactory assault.

(f) Leave your cubicle and return when you think
your neighbor will be finished with his snack.

(g) Go buy your own to satisfy your craving.

ANSWERS:

(1) False. The first microwave oven was invented in 1946 by Dr.
Percy Spencer, a Raytheon Corporation employee. (2) "That's great,
Newton. I hope this turns out the way you hope it does." Though a
cubicle dweller should never be a doormat to other people's ideas
and opinions, when it comes to the kitchen and food, it is best to be
as relaxed, nonjudgmental, and flexible as possible. Serious trouble-
makers are instinctively ostracized and subtly punished by the community. (3) In order of preference:

(a) It is best to acknowledge how you are being affected
by the popcorn smell and be subtle about your desire to be given some.

(b) Cubicle dwellers appreciate directness and honesty,
as long as the delivery is polite.

(g) Popcorn is inexpensive and takes minutes to cook.
Be willing to lose some fights to win the war of cubicle survival.

(f) This option is viable but undesirable because it sacri-
fices productivity and forthrightness. Still, it may be
worth the blow to your backbone if it strengthens
your reputation and stock in the cubicle community.

(c) This approach is respectable because it is honest, but
lacks creativity and a general sense of tact or com-
passion.

(d) Don't lie to your cubicle mates, even about a small
matter like dieting. It will somehow, in some way,
come back to haunt you.

(e) This is an all-out assault on the perpetrator and total breakdown in the rules governing civilization on the cubicle farm. Be prepared to be fired at or, even worse, have your victim fire back. You've started a war by escalating the risks and rewards. No one can win.

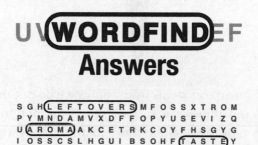

CHAPTER SIX
Hygiene

Human fear stems from things we do not understand and things we cannot see. Thus nothing spreads more trepidation through the cubicle community than a colleague's perplexing sanitary habits—or lack of sanitary habits and subsequent microscopic germs that jump around our bodies and office supplies like invisible fleas. We know to avoid sick colleagues who don't know when to stay home or how to sneeze properly, but how do we steer clear of co-workers who don't wash their hands after a bowel movement or those who lack an understanding of contemporary Western hygiene? Confronting these challenges is fraught with professional and social pitfalls. Fortunately, most situations can be diffused by carefully balancing tolerance, respect, and straightforwardness. Neither the messenger nor the recipient of such news wants to be embarrassed. From the outset remember that some dilemmas result from cultural differences, some from ignorance, and others from outright boorishness. Determining the intention or reason behind hygienic aggravations is essential to addressing the behavior and bringing it to a stop.

Hands

Germs and microbes are as much a part of the cubicle community as boredom, gossip, and 2 percent pay raises. Cooties are everywhere—especially on your hands. However, don't turn your cubicle into that makeshift government HAZ-MAT lab used to hold Spielberg's comically misunderstood E.T. Don't become a paranoid Howard Hughes disciple cowering in the corner of a Hollywood penthouse, wrapped in a heavily starched bedsheet screaming at invisible diseases. Chances are you do not shake hands with extraterrestrial life-forms when they see you in the hallway with a handful of Reese's Pieces. You probably don't share a stapler with a mumbling billionaire aviator in the cubicle next to you. Proper hand hygiene does not require you to wear rubber gloves and walk around as if you're going to cavity-search colleagues who return from the bathroom in less than three minutes. Don't be a hygiene vigilante. Germs, microbes, cooties, and bacteria are all part of normal life in the cubicle farm. So get used to it. Understand, however, that accepting their existence does not mean that you have to welcome them. Proper hand hygiene is key to continued health.

Bob Novack from finance uses the same fingers to type company quarterly reports, turn doorknobs, and refill the printer that he does to scratch his genitalia, pop zits in the rearview mirror during a lull in the morning rush hour, and yank out unruly nose hairs when he has the elevator to himself. Believe it or not, Bob Novack is a normal employee. Imagine what the crazies in your office do with their hands when no one is looking. For your own protection, employ what you learned in chapter 4 by washing your hands regularly with soap and hot water and keeping antibacterial tissues or lotion handy. Avoid

CUBERS
INTERNATIONAL

BUILDING A BETTER TOMORROW

HANDWASHING
THE CUBERS WAY

1

Turn on water to a comfortable temperature and moisten hands and wrists.

2

Apply a generous portion of liquid soap.

3

Generate a heavy lather and wash well for approx. 15 seconds. Clean between fingers, nail beds, under fingernails, and backs of hands.

4

Rinse well under running water, keeping hands low in sink to prevent splashing.

5

Hold hands so that water flows from the wrist to fingertips.

6

Dry hands completely with clean paper towels.

7

Use the paper towel to turn off the faucet so your hands remain clean.

hand-to-hand contact with people you suspect of poor hand hygiene and refrain from using the same office supplies or touching the same surfaces they do. Still, do all of these things discreetly and without insulting others by implying they are unsanitary. If necessary, explain that you are a garden-variety neurotic when it comes to germs and that they in no way should take your actions personally. However, it is always important for members of the cubicle community to be honest when it comes to individual standards regarding protocol, including and especially hygiene protocol. Otherwise, the path of white lies, attempts to spare others humiliation, and saving face can lead entire departments into a vortex of conspiracy, manipulation, and coercion.

Jonathon Nogel is the executive vice president of Cubers

International. Jonathon is admired throughout his profession for his business savvy, market analysis acumen, and moderate good looks (average height, blond hair, blue eyes, but an unfortunate case of red cheek that spreads like spilled wine as his level of social discomfort increases—especially around attractive women). Jonathon "decided" early in life—his freshman year at the University of North Carolina—that his future would be better served by focusing on his academic and financial goals rather than pursuing women or social activities. One Saturday night while Jonathon played Internet chess against shipmate2764b, a retired fifty-two-year-old female deckhand in Portland, Oregon, he announced to his opponent that he needed a fifteen-minute respite in order to use the bathroom. "Taco Bell," he succinctly explained. While perched on the toilet seat and reading the sports section of the campus newspaper, Jonathon had a revelation and, upon returning to the cyber chess match, defeated the lesbian deckhand in one brilliant move.

From that night forward Jonathon consulted the nearest toilet whenever he found himself in need of inspiration— which, at Cubers International, was a daily event, usually in the morning. Before turning down the hallway toward the bathroom, Jonathon would stride past his assistant's cubicle and into the kitchen, where he would scan the reading table that offered employees free copies of the most recent daily newspapers and weekly magazines. Jonathon would then grab whichever publication struck his fancy at the moment and head off to the toilet; there he'd contemplate the latest celebrity breakups, sports scores, and political headlines while mulling over his professional challenges of the day. Then he would fold the paper, lay it on the floor, and leisurely commence wiping. Twenty minutes later he would stride by his assistant's cubicle, into the kitchen to replace the publication, and thence to his corner office.

That's when Lindsay Burchette, his assistant of four years, would walk out of her cubicle and attach a small Post-it note to whichever publication she noticed he had taken into the bathroom. On the Post-it note was scrawled "C" so her colleagues would know which piece of literature to avoid reading during their lunch breaks. The "C," of course, stood for "contaminated." Though Lindsay Burchette was very loyal to her boss, she was just as loyal to her colleagues. They, after all, insisted it was Lindsay's duty to either tell her boss that his conduct was "gross and unhygienic" or somehow let them know which kitchen reading materials were unfit for human contact. Lindsay came up with the Post-it solution three days after the confrontation. To this day Lindsay Burchette remains well liked by her boss and colleagues.

Fingernails

In the cubicle community clean and well-groomed fingernails are a sign of fastidiousness, attention to detail, and self-respect. Men should have smooth, round fingernails with clean cuticles and no visible dirt or grime. Women should maintain filed nails and indulge in the socially odd but very acceptable option to decorate them, even if that requires dressing up each individual fingernail like a flamboyant samba dancer at Mardi Gras in Rio. In fact, many women use their fingernails as platforms on which to strut their only opportunity at individualism and self-expression within the confines of corporate policy. Some even go for the versatile and formidable fake-fingernail option, which often comes in the form of "press-ons." These women can be heard typing in their cubicles from several hundred yards away. Additionally, fake nails can be used as letter openers, as slim-jims in case you lock your keys in your car, or as plastic knives to cut cake when the company runs out of utensils at office birthday and going-away parties. To the ignorant, long pimped-out fingernails may look difficult to manage and inefficient, but it doesn't take much time to learn how to type and remove staples several feet from your desk. For ideas on how women can make their fake fingernails more colorful, loud, and sparkly, visit your local Department of Motor Vehicles or US Post Office, or catch the latest Dolly Parton video on Country Music Television. Long fake fingernails are also hygienic because they reduce the contact surface area. It's like walking around on stilts, except you wear them on your hands.

In the cubicle community clean fingernails are good, but cleaning your fingernails is bad. In fact, it's revolting. Cutting your fingernails in your cubicle is seen as an early step in an uncivilized march toward bringing private bathroom behavior into the cubicle community. And don't think you can get away with it because no one is looking. The human senses inherently train themselves to detect threatening and suspiciously out-of-place noises. War veterans can never shake the terror of hearing a branch snap in the still of night. Sleep-weary truck drivers jolt to attention when something goes thump beneath their tires. Spouses freeze when they hear their friend's voice coming from the bedroom. Cubicle dwellers glower when the click of a severed fingernail pierces the office humdrum. They wait in silence. *This can't be real. Rodney graduated third in his class. His wife is a sophisticated food critic. He calls everyone "sir" and "ma'am." He would never . . . Click. The horror. It can't be. Click . . . click.*

Fingernails are disgusting, which is why women should decorate them more than their bedrooms and men should clean them more than their cars. They require maintenance because they are ugly. Fake fingernails are popular because unlike fake hair and fake teeth, replacement fingernails are not trying to compensate for the absence of something. Fake fingernails acknowledge that the wearer's actual fingernails are so ugly that they had to be filed down like rusted roofing nails and replaced with bright plastic blades the size of tongue depressors.

Click. That is the sound of nasty, repulsive fingernail bits being shot around your neighbor's cubicle the way a lawn mower spits out a box turtle. Cutting fingernails in a cubicle is wrong. However, cubicle dwellers who do it suffer from delusional complacency, unmitigated self-absorption, or the ever-expanding pandemic of cube denial wherein they believe, for some reason, that their colleagues cannot hear or figure out what they are doing. Cube denial is a powerful affliction; the symptoms can lie dormant for years, then suddenly manifest themselves. The slightest trigger can instantly turn the most self-conscious and considerate employees into fingernail butchers, flinging fingernail shrapnel in all directions, including over the cube walls and into the open space behind them. Much as with drug addicts and their crack pipes, heroin syringes, and track marks, it is difficult to hide the process of nail cutting. Though many try to convince themselves they can do it without getting caught, they usually end up in trouble with the cubicle law enforcement or, worse, out on the streets. Remember one simple rule: Keep bathroom behavior in *your* bathroom. Otherwise there may come a day when a colleague takes a dump on your desk and claims that it belongs to a friend.

Employees who bite their own fingernails are a distressing bunch. Many are addicted to the nail-biting habit and have a way of making their peers uncomfortable and even nauseous. As with most addictions, chronic nail biters have two options: Get help or learn to function without indulging. Employees who just can't stop biting their nails should realize how disgusting the habit is to their colleagues, and how this could have a negative influence on their job security. Nail biters must mitigate the fallout of their behavior, especially in the cubicle. They should never allow nail biting to be audible; they must ensure that the gnawed-off pieces of fingernail are immediately dispensed of so that colleagues never see them. Though it is impossible to hide the evidence of nail biting on the tips of the fingers, an addicted nail biter can create the impression that they chomp on their cuticles only at home. Cubicle residents who can no longer tolerate a neighbor's nail-biting habits should compassionately voice their concerns to the offender, or, when no one is looking, leave a tube of that nasty nail-biting-cessation cream on their neighbor's cubicle chair.

Feet

The only thing that separates us from Planet Earth is our feet, and there is a lot that can go wrong between the floor and our ankles. Common burdens include athlete's foot and other fungi, muscle aches, stubbed toes, corns, gangrene, fallen arches, broken bones, frostbite, yellowing toenails, itches, bunions, arthritis, turf toe, and heel spurs. One or a combination of these afflictions may cause cubicle residents to believe that it is necessary, or indeed okay, to take off their shoes. There is never, ever a justification for removing your shoes at your cubicle, even if you are the Incredible Hulk and find your expanding green feet splitting the seams of your loafers apart. Head for the elevator and get outside. Find some bushes to hide in. Then, only then, is it okay to remove your shoes. Again, it's an issue concerning the slippery slope of cascading standards. If removing shoes becomes acceptable behavior in the cubicle community, then what is to stop employees from removing their shirts to refresh their armpits or removing their pants to make trips to the restroom more efficient?

Also, feet stink. Shannon Grimm in cubicle 7-A at the programming department wears expensive perfume, manicures her eyebrows every morning, and gets monthly Botox injections to hide the V of blue veins that emerges from her forehead whenever she becomes stressed or frustrated, which is all the time. Her unchecked sense of vanity developed so uncontrollably over the years that her obsession with visual appearances and superficialities actually took over the part of her brain that controls her sense of smell. Unfortunately for Shannon's colleagues, she thinks no one knows that she often kicks off her pumps while working at her cubicle to air out her feet, which smell like a mix of blue cheese salad dressing and motor oil. Not even the panty hose she wears in the winter months impede the stench that oozes from the bottoms of her feet and between her toes. Summertime is even worse, for Shannon loves sandals, particularly her rope sandals with the interwoven seashells. When her colleagues leave work and break off into cliquey happy hours, they refer to her as "Shannon Grimm with feet of a hippo."

Somewhere an unfortunate trend developed in the evolution of corporate fashion for males: the modern-day work sock. Unlike athletic socks, which are thick, cushioned, absorbent, and offered in a variety of styles and colors, work socks are thin, uncomfortable, drab, and so constrictive that they leave the imprint of the knitting on men's ankles and squashed leg hairs. At the end of the day men's ankles look like Roman columns. Work socks feel as if they are made from fabric plastic wrap. So it is no surprise that Thomas Boone kicks off his shoes and socks at his cubicle. Even though at his back is a seldom traveled hallway, his cubicle street is well aware that he is going commando with his feet. At first no one notices, but then as Thomas begins scratching his feet and scouring the lint from between his toes, the odor rises like smoke from a twig-wielding Boy Scout working on his Fire Safety merit badge. As Thomas's feet enjoy the touch of fresh air, his colleagues begin e-mailing one another, gathering a consensus and drafting a complaint that they will submit to their boss and human resource department requesting some sort of corporate intervention. Three days after the complaint is submitted, Thomas Boone storms out of the building, repeatedly describing the situation as "f—ing bulls—t." The next day he sends his wife to

clean his cubicle and pack his things in an old ramen soup cardboard box.

Body Odor

Many people think that body odor was eradicated about
the same time the feudal system was deemed no
longer effective as a way to organize human beings. Though
today serfs no longer have to pay fiefs and castles are little
more than tourist traps where wealthy newlyweds spend their
honeymoons, body odor is still very much a part of human existence. In fact, entire commercial industries have garnered
billions selling products that combat and even subdue unwanted body smells. If it weren't for breakthroughs in both
technology and hygienic standards, the modern-day cubicle
would probably be three times as spacious, allowing room for
odors to ventilate. Nevertheless, there are still some out there
who smell as if they haven't bathed since King John signed the
Magna Carta in 1215. How can this be? No one really knows
what smelly people are thinking. Do they know they smell and
just not care? Or do they have no idea that they smell? Don't
they have loved ones to inform them that they smell? Don't
they realize that being smelly in the cubicle community is not
only a professional death wish but also a major aggravation for
co-workers? How, after all, do you politely and professionally
tell someone they stink? Really. How can you not know you
smell? It's like being on fire. The answer is simple: People are
weird, and cubicle communities, for better or worse, are inhabited by people. Accept reality. Body odor is a prevalent
issue in the office. So how to combat the smelly person's
smells? Most people try to be understanding and develop
various means of neutralizing, smothering, or deflecting the
odors. Most fight smell with smell.

Halitosis, Untended Teeth, and Onion Breath

Inevitably cubicle dwellers will have to share their space with one or more colleagues in order to work on a particular project or assignment. When this happens colleagues learn intimate things about one another, such as what the others ate for lunch, whether or not they brush their teeth, and how many cups of coffee they have had. Though these are temporary inconveniences, they can be very uncomfortable, distracting, and unfortunately repeated often. In the event that you find yourself cramped in your cubicle and staring at PowerPoint slides on your computer with an office mate, be prepared. If your co-worker has breath that smells like garlic, or has rotting flesh caught in his teeth, or is on a no-carb diet and exhales urine vapors, keep a bowl of mints at your desk and offer—insist, if necessary—that they partake of your hospitality. Have an assortment of nice-smelling snacks or sweets just in case your colleagues don't care for a particular variety.

Farts

It is almost impossible to write the word *fart* without seeming sophomoric or juvenile; however, the expression, like the experience, is a necessary evil. People fart every day, and there isn't a word in the English language or scientific community that better describes the event than the word *fart*. Political correctness needs to take a backseat on this one. So does unwarranted judgment. Farts happen. It is important to recognize the difference between accidental farting and pathological farting. Whether silent or audible, accidental farts are embarrassing and beyond one's control, like falling down the steps. They should be forgiven. Whether silent or audible, habitual farts are inexcusable. They should not be forgiven. Serial farters have either a psychological or a physical problem that needs to be addressed. Consult with your human resource department for the best way to do this. You don't want to accuse colleagues of being disrespectful, immature, and vulgar when they are in fact suffering from a physical ailment. Resolve the problem without jumping to conclusions. In the meantime, use the techniques in this chapter to combat the flatulence. Be less uptight when it comes to run-of-the-mill farting. Deal with the smell but go on with your work life as if nothing happened. Follow a *Don't say, don't smell* policy.

Don't ask Omar in the corner cubicle, "Something smells like burning tires. Did you let one rip?" If Omar says no, most people will think he is lying—and he has nothing to gain by answering that question honestly. So let it go. If you are the one who lets an inadvertent fart rip, do the best you can to get away with it. If it is silent, let it drift into the jumbled memories of your past like a bad haircut. If the fart is audible, turn in your chair so that it makes noises, open and close a few drawers as if you're looking for something, or fumble with some office supplies. Do something that might cloak the sound of your fart by making it sound like just another random noise in a series of noises. If the fart noise is obviously a fart and nothing else, either admit culpability by getting up and going to the bathroom, or be stoic and anxiously wait for the social fallout like a child in the principal's office. Truly professional cubicle communities know the difference between a criminal behavior and human necessities.

Perfume, Deodorant, and Cologne Abuse

Perfume, deodorants, and cologne, like Jägermeister, should be applied sparingly, responsibly, and with utmost caution. These products are addictive, and some people can't control themselves around their intoxicating effects. Despite what you may feel and think, they don't make you better-looking. In fact, men and women who don't know when

Fragrance Tap

they've had enough often make fools of themselves in front of everyone. No one likes to be around folks who can't control their smell-enhancement use. Men and women in cubicle communities often stagger around the workplace in a self-induced morphine-like haze of perfume and cologne. It's not good for the lungs, either. In their minds they think the handsome UPS deliveryman is flirting uncontrollably by asking for a signature, or that the sexy new woman in management training looks at her shoes while she walks because she's too smitten to make eye contact. In reality smell-enhancement addicts are actual human versions of the Pigpen character in Charles Schulz's *Peanuts* cartoon. Yes, the dirty one ensconced in a brown cloud that pulsates and follows every step he takes. Unfortunately, smell-enhancement abuse remains socially acceptable; to this day there are no formal treatment programs or clinics where abusers can seek help to educate and reform themselves. Until society comes around and sees smell-enhancement abuse for the human tragedy that it is, countless Americans will continue to walk through life, and between cubicles, sauced on French fragrances and exotic odors that make everyone nearby nauseous, convulsive, and saddened by lost human potential.

Take Kathy Valencia. Every weekday morning the recently divorced archive video specialist from Burlington, Vermont, wakes up at 6:45 AM sharp before heading out to Cubers International. In her ironed bathrobe, she eats half a cantaloupe carefully cut into cubes and watches the *Today* show. Kathy likes the *Today* show because they talk about relationships and divorce more than other networks. Afterward she takes a lukewarm shower and washes her hair with three ounces of aloe-and-avocado shampoo and one ounce of creamy guava conditioner. Kathy splashes her face three times with an organic moisturizing "system" that costs $38.95 a bottle. Her work clothes are hanging in a closet wrapped in plastic, fresh from a biweekly trip to the dry cleaners. Though Kathy's attention to detail makes her a natural archivist and valued employee at Cubers International, it also contributed to her husband's departure. Her ex-husband explained, while pulling out of the driveway with a car full of stereo equipment, that she has "the mind and the personality of a database."

Kathy spent that evening crying on the toilet, querying her mind for examples of spontaneity and outlandish behavior in her life. Wiping tears from her face with a fistful of toilet paper, she eventually conceded, "Sorry, no matches found." Kathy vowed to be a different person, to be less programmed, to be rebellious. The next morning, while eating cantaloupe cubes and watching the *Today* show, Kathy witnessed a black-and-white commercial that showed a beautiful woman in sunglasses smiling uncontrollably and driving a convertible as her hair swirled in the air. A sultry voice entered the commercial. "Cheating husband," it said. Suddenly the woman and the convertible ran over something sizable, abruptly rising and falling within the camera shot. Then the scene faded to a sleek spray bottle of perfume with a single word elegantly written in cursive across it: REBELLION. The sultry voice returned. "For women tired of not fighting back."

During her lunch break Kathy bought five spray bottles of Rebellion for a total of $262.57. For the next several weeks, after adjusting her hair in the bathroom mirror, Kathy sprayed her body with Rebellion as if she were a cleaning a sliding glass door with Windex. Everyone in her cubicle neighborhood knew that Kathy's husband had left and that she was going through a difficult time. In the beginning her co-workers were sympathetic to her situation and did their best to neutralize her overwhelming aroma. Many bought small rotating fans that they clicked on whenever she walked past. Some secretly burned scented candles after stopping by to inquire about some business matter. Others simply covered their noses and mouths with paper towels, tissues, or other types of fabric. One co-worker even bought a stack of surgical masks and explained that she was "allergic to certain molds, weeds, and fumes." Kathy Valencia soon transformed from a popular and well-respected employee to an unpopular and tragic example of smell-enhancement-product abuse.

It wasn't until months passed that one of Kathy's colleagues realized that her friend in a copier supply company worked with a man who abused cologne. Kathy and the cologne man went out on a blind date at TGI Friday's. The two were seated at a narrow table in a musty corner of the restaurant. Before they even had a chance to order drinks their respective fuming aromas violently interacted with each other like bleach and ammonia, creating a noxious, milky gas that sent both to the floor, where they convulsed like a pair of frogs in a microwave. Ten minutes later paramedics whisked them off on stretchers to Saint Jude's Hospital. After three weeks of physical therapy and emotional counseling, Kathy was back at her cubicle. Her blind date was also released but soon afterward he was arrested for exposing himself to potted geraniums at a plant nursery. He was never heard from again. Though Kathy got her job back, her professional reputation was ruined forever. She eventually wrote a bestselling book about her addiction to Rebellion and later told America about her experiences while being interviewed on the *Today* show.

Anti-Smell Tactics and Arsenal

As briefly noted in the cautionary tale above, cubicle workers have developed some innovative and effective devices for combating intense stenches and unhygienic odors in the cubicle community. Many fight unwelcome smells with an arsenal of eco-terrorist-friendly fragrances such as mountain pine, country scent, rose petal, wintergreen, wild berries, spring rain, vanilla blossom, potpourri, roasted almonds, mixed bouquets, lemon fresh, and other citrus. There are various means of dispensing these smells. Spray pumps and aerosol cans are the most common. They also make distinct sounds when being used. Spray-pump bottles are relatively low-key and release a focused, heavier discharge of floral-scented molecules perfect for neutralizing infected areas of carpet or establishing a perimeter of good smell. Dogs use this same principle on fire hydrants and tree trunks to mark their personal territory. The dense spray settles in a concentrated rain that can fume for hours, creating an invisible force field of good smell.

Aerosol cans release a highly compressed streaming burst of molecules, like a mini space shuttle booster rocket. They can be deployed much like Ronald Reagan's famous Star Wars defense shield: Threatening missiles such as farts, wafts of body odor, or exhales of bad breath can be safely intercepted and neutralized in the atmosphere. Aerosol cans are also effective against migratory infusions of bad smell from ambulant colleagues and gangsta-style stinky-people drive-bys and muggings. Furthermore, cubicle dwellers can make a social statement by producing a small but tactful scene whenever they feel the need to defend themselves against intrusive body odors. Fumigating your cubicle with a can of lavender meadow air freshener mere seconds after a colleague departs will undoubtedly cause your neighbors and the smelly perpetrator to turn their heads. If everyone in a cubicle community adopted this policy, even the most boneheaded perpetrator would eventually figure it out. However, whenever people learn something undesirable about themselves, they often direct their anger toward the messenger. So be careful. When defending your hygienic standards, your cubicle space, and even your own sanity, be prepared to confront the situation honestly but diplomatically. Take into account what your colleagues must be feeling. For example, consider the following conversations.

Anti-Smell Conversation, Version 1
Cubicle 56-M, Fifth Floor. 3:12 PM.

Mary: Doug, I think my highlighter is stuck to your wrist.

Doug: Whoa! Looky that!

Mary: I know you're busy with work and personal life stuff. It must be nice to be so active and on the go. However, I think the highlighter is stuck to the sweaty, greasy film on your skin. Maybe you should take a break from being so busy and take a shower tonight. With soap. It's a good way to relax.

Doug: Nah. I've got karate class tonight and then hot yoga tomorrow morning. No time for showering.

Mary: Okay. Would you mind if we finished this project in the conference room? That table is huge. I can sit on one side and you can sit on the other side. That way we will have plenty of space to work.

Doug: Well, I guess. It kind of seems like a waste of time, but if you need to spread out these portfolios, we can do that. I'm pretty flexible.

Mary: Well, I hear yoga is all about flexibility. Thanks, Doug. Oh, here. Can you take this handful of sanitized Handi Wipes with you? I can't carry them with all of these folders.

Doug: Uh. Okay.

Mary: Thanks! Oh, you go ahead. I've got one more thing to do here. I'll meet you in the conference room in about five minutes. You go ahead.

Doug: Whatever. See you there.

Aerosol Can of Marigold Meadow: *Shhhhh. Chhhhhhh. Shhhh. Chhhh. Chhhhhh. Shhhhhhh. Shhhhh. Shhh-hhh. Chhhhhh. Shhhhhh. Chh.*

Anti-Smell Conversation, Version 2
Cubicle 56-M, Fifth Floor. 3:12 PM.

Mary: Doug, I think my highlighter is stuck to your wrist.

Doug: Whoa! Looky that!

Mary: I know you're busy with work and personal life stuff. It must be nice to be so active and on the go. However, I think the highlighter is stuck to the sweaty, greasy film on your skin. Maybe you should take a break from being so busy and take a shower tonight. With soap. It's a good way to relax.

Doug: Nah. I've got karate class tonight and then hot yoga tomorrow morning. No time for showering.

Mary: Okay. Would you mind closing your eyes and holding this Handi Wipe over your nose?

Doug: Huh?

> **Mary.** Oh, come on. Just do it. This is important to our business objectives.
>
> **Doug:** Well, fine.
>
> **Mary:** I see you peeking. Close your eyes tight.
>
> **Aerosol Can of Marigold Meadow:** *Shhhhh. Chhhhhh. Shhhh. Chhhh. Chhhhhh. Shhhhhhh. Shhhhh. Shhhhhh. Chhhhhh. Shhhhhh. Chh.*

Many members of the cubicle community choose a maintenance-type approach that requires a lower-level but more sustained use of munitions. These employees do not experience concentrated odorous assaults to their cubicle space, but suffer from a more sustained, hovering form of stench that is part of the climate, like smog in Los Angeles. They have sanitary neighbors, for instance, but their neighbors' neighbors may exude body odor; or they may be situated near a smelly bathroom or kitchen. Strategies to defuse lingering odors are myriad. Leaving an open stick of deodorant in a discreet location in one's cubicle is a wise approach. Uncapped deodorant sticks emit a steady, subtle, clean smell that does a great job of counteracting odors without dominating the cubicle atmosphere with musk or fresh-scent antiperspirant.

Plug-in air fresheners are also gaining in popularity because they spurt fresh scents on a timed schedule. They are reliable, out of the way, and self-regulated. Also, plug-in air fresheners come in a dazzling variety of scents that sound more like lounge drinks on a Carnival cruise ship, "Tropical Mist Potpourri" and "Hawaiian Breeze."

For the hip and economical seeking to "pimp" their cubicle, the pine-tree-shaped air freshener commonly found dangling from the rearview mirrors of muscle cars and ghetto cruisers is a stylish way to go. They come in the classic choices of "Freedom Tree," "Spiced Patchouli," and "Vanillaroma." Pine-tree-shaped air fresheners can be purchased at any rural or ghetto Exxon station for $1.89. Schlitz and Colt 45 sold separately.

Quick Quiz Self-Assessment

(1) Amy Milmo is alone in her cubicle but on a conference call with four other people—three subcontractors from Plethora Fabrics spread across the Midwest and a very important client in Chicago who represents a major retail chain. Amy is a regional manager at Cubers International and holds seniority in the gathering. Cubers International is synergizing into retail. While discussing the resurgence of polyester in lower-end market sales, Amy hears a clicking sound over the intercom. It's Harold Wheeler, Plethora Fabrics' new research-and-development guy; he's obviously cutting his nails.

"What's that clicking sound?" the client asks.

"I'm not sure," Amy says, buying time to think of a reasonable explanation.

"Nothing!" Harold blurts. "It's nothing. Maybe somebody's watch."

"Anyway," Amy jumps in, "about the new polyester weave for our outdoor line . . ."

The clicking continues.

"What *is* that?" says Lucy Wagner, Plethora Fabrics' finance officer in Boise, Idaho.

"Nothing!" shouts Harold.

"It sounds like someone is clipping their nails!" the client remarks. "Is someone clipping their nails? That's gross."

"No one is clipping their nails!" Harold insists. "It's probably someone tapping their ring on a desk or something."

"I don't wear a ring," the client says. "I'm single. Ugh. There just aren't any good men in this town."

Click. Click.

"Whoever is doing that, stop it now," Amy demands. "Now, our new weave offers twice the comfort for . . ."

Click.

"Stop it, Harold!"

"It's not me!"

"The hell it's not you! I can practically see the dirt in your fingers over the phone line!"

"Everyone calm down," says Lucy.

"Harold, do you have a girlfriend?" the client asks.

"Even if it was me," Harold retorts, "what could you do about it, Amy? You don't have any proof."

"I could have you fired," Amy says.

"Harold?" murmurs the client.

"I'm seeing someone," says Harold. "A *model*."

"Really?" says Lucy. "You don't sound like a *model* type of guy. I don't believe you."

Click. The client hangs up.

"What the hell is a *model* type of guy supposed to sound like? Huh?" Harold shouts.

"That's it!" Amy screams. "I'm going to _____

(a) contact Harold's manager and have him fired. Then I'm going to call our client and apologize and beg for her business back. Lucy, good-bye. Harold, pack your bags!"

(b) call our client and get her back on the line. You two stay patched in and don't go anywhere. Harold, if I hear one more *click*, you're fired."

(c) quit this job. Dealing with you idiots isn't worth all the money in the world. Good-bye, assholes."

(d) hang up and chastise myself for being unprofessional because no one should ever conduct a conference call from a cubicle."

(e) b and c.

(f) a and b.

(g) c and d.

(h) a and d.

(i) a and c.

(2) Carl Basil works in the middle of a cubicle street in the retirement benefits division of Cubers International, comprised of seventy-two employees. While crunching numbers in Microsoft Excel and accidentally clicking on the wrong function—again—he farts. It's about as loud as a winter jacket zipper being quickly unzipped and about as smelly as a mouse that's been dead for three days. In other words, his colleagues could hear the fart and in mere seconds they will be able to smell it, too. What should Carl Basil do to save face and protect his reputation as a consummate professional?

(a) Quietly excuse himself and walk to the bathroom so his colleagues know there won't be any more farts dropped in their vicinity.

(b) Remain quiet and pretend nothing happened, implying that farting is a natural bodily function and that these things happen. No big deal.

(c) Begin twisting in his chair, open and close his desk drawers, and loudly staple everything in sight as a cover for the original fart noise.

(d) Shout to his colleagues, "My bad! No use pretending it didn't happen!"

(e) Shout, "Damn, Keith!"—blaming the incident on the colleague he likes the least.

(3) True or False? Body odor is a natural phenomenon that has only been considered unappealing and unhealthy since 1388, when England began its violent persecution of the Loyolaists, a sect of Catholics steeped in the traditions of humility, piety, and grace. The Loyolaists believed that

cleansing the spirit meant denying the body any superficial satisfactions, including food, sex, and baths. In an effort to make them seem ridiculous and fanatical, the English Crown created an atmosphere of fear by spreading rumors that people who didn't bathe themselves didn't have souls and were nothing more than farm animals.

ANSWERS:
(1) h. Answer (a) is appropriate because Harold is a liar, unprofessional, and unhygienic—even on the phone. Answer (d) fits because Amy was indeed being unprofessional by conducting a conference call from her cubicle. (2) Answer (a) is best, though (b) is also acceptable. Answer (a) is apt because leaving the area infers that Carl understands the seriousness of what he did and wants his colleagues to understand that they are safe from further smelly assaults. Answer (b) would be acceptable because sometimes drawing attention to something makes it more apparent and threatening than it was to begin with. (3) False. Body odor is still alive and well today.

CHAPTER SEVEN

Entertaining Guests and Unannounced Visitors

Visiting Hours

In some cultures it's fine to just show up at some friends' apartment on a Saturday afternoon or your uncle and aunt's house on a Tuesday evening without notice. The surprised hosts will drop everything and break out food, drink, and pleasant conversation. The unannounced visitors will partake of their hospitality and not think twice about being a possible inconvenience. Good for those cultures. Now welcome to America. Call first. Make plans. Confirm them. Give others time to prepare their homes and themselves. Most of us are too busy earning a living to put dirty dishes in the dishwasher, comb our hair, and pick the kids' toys off the carpet. Showing up uninvited often leads to uncomfortable situations wherein the surprised hosts are embarrassed about the way things look and visitors feel like asses (and they should) for thinking *Who wouldn't want us to stop by right now? After all, it's us.* America invented the cubicle, and American corporate culture is the law of the land in cubicle communities. Learn the rules.

No Sneaking

Knock, fake-sneeze, say hello. Don't sneak up on people. Don't hover. Don't linger. Whenever you approach colleagues' cubicles—for whatever reason—always, *always,* make sure they know you are there. If you don't, your colleagues will (rightly) assume that you are spying on them, trying to get a glimpse of their computer monitors or listen in on their phone conversations. Make your presence known. It's not difficult, nor is it rude. Most cubicles have a wooden or steel slat on the partition that is as close as employees get to an actual door. So treat that slat as a door. Knock on it when visiting. If for some reason you can't or don't want to knock, then do something else to make your presence known. Though cubicle dwellers do have a well-developed sixth sense about what goes on behind them, don't rely on it and approach without warning. When all else fails, talk. Say "hello" or "excuse me." But don't just stand there. People who stand around and do nothing are creepy and dubious, like men who lack the courage to ask out women and torpidly stare at them instead. So avoid acting like a stalker and advertise your presence and intentions when visiting a colleague. Don't hover. Don't show up unannounced. Don't arrive without a purpose. However, if you do visit colleagues because you are bored, make sure your hosts have free time to waste with you. Leave them alone if they are busy. Move on to someone else or find a way to entertain yourself. Good cubicle guests know not to wear out their welcome.

The Office Lamprey

Every office has an odd-looking employee who swims around the cubicle community, latches onto unsuspecting colleagues, and sucks their patience dry before moving on to the next cubicle. This individual is known as the office lamprey. An actual lamprey is an aggressive parasite that resembles an eel but employs a round, razor-sharp-tooth-filled mouth that flares out and fastens onto a host fish. An anticoagulant in the lamprey's saliva allows it to siphon the life out of its prey for hours or weeks or until the host dies.

It has taken centuries for the waterbound lamprey to evolve into the modern-day office lamprey, but during that time it has proven a highly adaptable and formidable species. Modern office lampreys have adjusted their feeding cycles to avoid suspicion from their superiors by rotating from one cubicle host to the next, never sucking specific hosts to death, but depleting their reserves of patience and tolerance to the point of irritated confrontation or absolute exhaustion. Office lampreys ingratiate themselves with unsuspecting colleagues by bearing the latest news, stock quotes, weather reports, and inane personal stories involving lawn care, child rearing, or underwear purchases. However, before the host employee realizes what has happened, it is too late. The office lamprey has attached itself. Firmly. It won't let go. There is no getting out of a conversation with an office lamprey. Office lampreys are finely tuned soul-sucking machines. Only after the office lamprey detects a supervisor or other danger does it cease talking and retract its grip on the host employee.

Office lampreys know not to exploit a particular host for too long, for they run the risk of gaining the unwanted attention of their bosses or the wrath of their colleagues. For office

Office Lamprey

Pronunciation: (lam'prē), [key]
—n.,
—pl. -preys.

Defined as: Any parasitic,
eel-like land mammal with a
suctorial mouth and horny teeth
used for boring into the flesh of
other team members to feed on
their blood.

Family: *Petro-intrudus uninvitus*
Length: 60 – 74 inches
Weight: 1,500 – 2,220 ounces
Coloring: gray-blue back, metallic
violet on sides, shading to silver-white
underneath
Common Names: great cube lamprey,
office lamprey, lamprey, lamprey eel
Found in: cubicle farms of corporations
both large and small

lampreys to survive, they must feed off many different hosts in the cubicle community, not just one or two. Despite the speed of their evolutionary progress, most office lampreys, including the common North American office lamprey, have not mastered contemporary grooming techniques or dress skills. In fact, many dress like game-show hosts and wear toupees that clash with their natural hair color. Researchers at the University of Ohio claim that the office lamprey's inability to camouflage itself and blend in with its environment may lead to its extinction.

Thus, even though office lampreys seem to be everywhere, they are actually a threatened species and protected by the Corporate Endangered Species Act of 1977. Only one out of seventeen cubicle workers is an office lamprey. Harming or even threatening an office lamprey is against the law, and cubicle neighborhoods across America have reluctantly learned to live with them, the way Alaskans do with grizzly bears. The situation remains a balancing act between nature and the encroaching needs of civilization.

The Arizona National Zoo has even opened an office lamprey exhibit complete with cubicles and a sparsely furnished kitchen; the exhibit features both a male named Eugene Paulson and a female named Zelda Armstrong. Zoo officials are trying to get them to mate, but the male seems to have no game and the female no sex drive. They may resort to in vitro fertilization. The Chinese Grand Zoo of Animals in Beijing has already expressed interest in adopting one for its own office lamprey restoration project. Though the office lamprey may be a threatened species, they are, like the Bengal tiger, dangerous and to be avoided.

So how do cubicle dwellers protect themselves from office lampreys and other unwanted and potentially hazardous visitors?

Defensive Body-Language and Positioning Techniques

Don't make eye contact. Whatever you do, don't make eye contact. Treat unwelcome visitors the same way you would a man on the street wearing a scuba mask, oven mitts, and a sequined blouse. Stare at your feet. Scratch an imaginary bug bite. Play with the hair on your arms. Just don't look at them no matter how intrigued or scared you may feel. Once eye contact is made, you have established confirmation of each other's existence, and anything that happens after that point is a reaction that can't be explained away by "I didn't know you were there" or "I didn't see you." Crazy people don't attack people; they attack situations. Don Quixote didn't attack windmills because he thought they were monsters. Don Quixote attacked windmills because he thought they were monsters *that* *were looking at him.* Once you acknowledge the unwanted visitor with a meeting of the eyes, it's too late to swivel back around in your chair or begin shuffling papers as if nothing has happened. Ask any woman who has been to happy hour at the local bar. If she, even for a second, makes eye contact with the man nearby staring at her through binoculars, the man will undoubtedly interpret this eye contact as *She thinks I'm a hot potato. She's checking out my hip cardboard hat. She wants me come over to talk to her.* The same rules apply in the cubicle community. If you make eye contact with an undesirable—an office lamprey, for instance—be prepared for an awkward and time-consuming conversation. Recover from your body-language mistake with emergency-response body language, effective word choice, and conversational manipulation. Consider the following examples.

Poor Choice of Office Lamprey Response
Cubicle 11-A, Twenty-second Floor. 10:44 AM.

Office Lamprey (adjusting toupee and silently standing at Betty's back as she types on her keyboard): Your kids need a ride.

Betty Markey (turning around and, unfortunately, making eye contact): Excuse me? Oh, Kenny. I didn't know it was you.

Office Lamprey (latching on, positioning razor-sharp teeth onto host): I was just thinking. If it snows a lot this winter, you'll probably have to take some time off to pick your kids up from school if classes are canceled.

Betty Markey (unguardedly begins spilling lifeblood as lamprey's anticoagulant takes effect): Well, Kenny, it's August. It's eighty-seven degrees outside. We don't even know if we'll get snow this winter. We'll cross that bridge when we get there.

Office Lamprey: It snowed last year.

Betty Markey: Yes, Kenny. It did. But that doesn't mean it will snow that much *this* year.

Office Lamprey: But you took an afternoon off last winter to pick up your kids.

Betty Markey (getting dizzy from loss of blood, makes desperate attempt to free herself): Kenny, I'm busy. What is your point?

Office Lamprey: All I'm saying is that you might have to pick your kids up from school this winter if it snows like last winter. You said you would cross that bridge when you get there, but really you've already crossed that bridge once. To get back you need to cross it again.

Betty Markey (sliding into delirium): Wha . . . ? Are you saying I need to cross over a bridge twice in order to be back where I was? Wouldn't that make me . . . huh?

Office Lamprey: To get your kids from school, yes, you would need to cross that bridge again like you did last winter. If it snows a lot.

Betty Markey (nearing unconsciousness): Winter? Isn't it summer? Kids. I'm confused.

Office Lamprey (sensing his host is losing life and no longer a good source of nourishment): Nothing. I'm just saying. Never mind. I'm going to go and talk to Andrew. He told me he has termites in his house.

Excellent Choice of Office Lamprey Response
Cubicle 11-A, Twenty-second Floor. 10:44 AM.

Office Lamprey (adjusting toupee and silently standing at Betty's back as she types on her keyboard): Your kids need a ride.

Betty Markey (internally questioning the origin of such an out-of-context statement): Hold on. I'm sorry. I'm just trying to finish this paragraph.

Office Lamprey (agitatedly stepping into Betty's cubicle space): I was just saying. Your kids need a ride home.

Betty Markey (realizing she is under attack by an office lamprey, and reducing her field of vision by leaning in so her face is only inches from her monitor): Oh, hey, Kenny. Let's see— "If you have any questions or concerns, please don't hesitate to . . ." No. Hold on, Kenny. "If you have concerns, please voice them anytime . . ." No. That's not it, either. What can I do for you, Kenny?

Office Lamprey: Your kids. The snow. They may need a . . .

Betty Markey (touching the computer screen with her finger): "If you are unhappy with any of our services or products, contact . . ." No, that's no good, either. Kenny, do you need something?

Office Lamprey: The snow, your kids' school . . .

Betty Markey (squinting and turning her back completely on the office lamprey): Aha. "If you would like to suggest any way we can improve our services to our customers . . ." What's that, Kenny? . . . "Please contact . . ."

Office Lamprey: Nothing. Never mind. I'm going to see what Andrew is doing.

Body language isn't just the way you walk or the way you sit; it is a sophisticated means of dealing with confrontations, assaults, and advances. Boxing has the upper cut and left hook. Wrestling has the dragon leg screw whip and flying headscissors. Sports such as boxing and wrestling are examples of body-language dialogue. Yoga is body language as a means of interacting with nature and your own spirit. Body language in the cubicle community is very important, especially when people find themselves on the defensive. Yoga has the cobra pose and the cat-cow stretch. Similarly, cubicle body-language positioning techniques also have some basic moves that every cubicle employee should master before entering the corporate arena.

GREEK SHOULDER BLOCK: Though the ancient Greeks have given modern civilization many gifts in the fields of architecture, politics, and art, perhaps their greatest gift to the world of business was derived from the Greek's most recognized creation, the Olympic Games. It was during the Olympic Games that a special style of wrestling was developed, Greco-Roman style, and with it the Greek Shoulder Block. Originally designed as a means of shifting body weight to heft an opponent over one's torso and onto the ground, this maneuver, when conducted from an office swivel chair, can today have the same effect on unwanted cubicle visitors. Whenever an undesirable visitor attempts to gain control of the cubicle interaction, immediately wrest command of the confrontation by employing aggressive body positioning. First, use your peripheral vision, hearing, and that cubicle sixth sense of "behindness" to pinpoint the exact location of the intruder. Then swivel in your chair so that the intruder's center of gravity lines up directly with the line of your spine. Next, lean forward as if feigning intense interest in whatever is on your computer screen (just like Betty Markey did in the second conversation above). Now, without losing the alignment of your spine against the unsolicited visitor, hunch your shoulders as if you're lost at sea and curling around a floating beach ball. Flex your shoulder muscles and simultaneously relax your waist and plant your feet to ensure mobility in your office swivel chair. If the intruder is talking or making noises, use your sixth sense to guide your body position—so that your spine remains constantly in a direct line with the approaching visitor. When she shifts, you shift and shoulder block. If she changes directions, you change directions and shoulder block. Just as in combat, if you know where your enemy is, you have the upper hand. Intruders such as office lampreys know this, so don't be fooled by silence. Get them to make a noise. Ask questions that require an answer but not a conversation. Exchanging words only encourages them. Spread packing peanuts around your cubicle to act as "location mines." Stay hunched. Stay unresponsive. If necessary, take the offensive. Without losing your tactical posture, suddenly back your chair up to see if you can run over the lamprey's toes. If you have some, inadvertently shoot air freshener at them. But don't stop realigning your shoulders, to throw them off their balance. Keep thrusting your shoulder to the left, to the right, and back to the left, as you look for a chink in the armor. Eventually, like a fox trying to eat a turtle, the intruder will become frustrated and discouraged and eventually move on to less challenging prey.

COLD WAR DIP: Also known in America as the A-Bomb Duck, or in Japan as the Earthquake Drop, this maneuver has been scaring grade school children for decades. However, once those children grow up and enter the corporate world, they realize how those lessons learned so many years ago are still valuable today. This move has it origins in catastrophe—namely, nuclear attacks and natural disasters. Millions of grade-schoolers learned that the best way to counter a hailstorm of nuclear bombs was to crouch under a school desk and lock their hands behind their heads. The exact same technique can be used to repel unwanted office visitors, though instead of locking your hands behind your head, pretend to tie your shoe or adjust computer wires. When executing the Cold War Dip in your cubicle, remember to confirm, with a question or quick glimpse, that the intruder has left before reemerging from under your desk.

Offensive Body-Language and Positioning Techniques

The best defense, they say, is a good offense. The following body-language techniques prey on the fears of most cubicle intruders, such as the office lamprey. As you will learn, uncontrollable gestures, tics, and quirks are an effective nonverbal way of communicating, *You will pay for talking to me.*

ROLLER-COASTER NECK SUPLEX: When you find yourself haunted by an unwanted visitor who insists on engaging in useless conversation, explain that you "didn't sleep well last night" and then, while gripping the arms of your chair, act as if you're on a roller coaster. Shake wildly and roll your neck (this is important, hence the name of the maneuver), thrusting your head from side to side. Then straighten up and reduce the intensity of the shaking. Continue normal conversation for fifteen seconds, as if everything is business as usual, then hop back on the roller coaster. Repeat this technique over and over until the unwanted guest leaves, even if it is to call an ambulance.

AMMONIA CLOUD BLINK: Most large-scale cubicle environments have a slow blinker, a fast blinker, a frequent blinker, and an infrequent blinker. Despite their eccentricities, these blinkers are quite common and, in many cases, more endearing than distracting. Unsynchronized blinking, however, is flat-out freaky. Add intensity to unsynchronized blinking and you have an anti-cubicle-intruder technique that will repel any surprise assault from bored colleagues. The key to the Ammonia Cloud Blink is making sure you do not blink in harmony while contorting your face as if you were involuntarily inhaling ammonia fumes. Scrunch your face tightly, quickly relax it, then blink your left eye several times. Carry on normal conversation for fifteen seconds. Then scrunch your face again as if you're breathing in a cloud of ammonia, relax it, and this time blink your right eye several times. Allow fifteen seconds for routine chat. Repeat this technique again and again as needed. Cubicle residents with a talent for acting may even be able to tear up at will; this, coupled with an exasperated fanning of the face, is an excellent embellishment to the Ammonia Cloud Blink technique.

INCOMPETENT CHAIR MECHANIC: No one likes to talk to someone who is obviously preoccupied with another deliberation or task. Not paying attention is disrespectful. However, many of us, particularly men, have developed the ability to inconspicuously disassociate during conversations, even while apparently engaged in a sincere and deep exchange of thoughts. In the cubicle community, preoccupation, taken to extremes, can be a very useful tool in the war on unwanted visitors. Make no attempts to hide your fixation. In fact, flaunt it. Obsess over your chair. Office chairs have long been an annoyance in the cubicle community. Research done by the online University of Carthage demonstrates that it takes newly hired employees "six or seven months to either adjust their office chair to the point that it is comfortable or successfully steal a pre-adjusted, comfortable chair from a colleague in the workplace." So stressing about the height, angle, lumbar support, or maneuverability of your office chair would not be considered irrational. Go for it.

Whenever unwelcome visitors stop by, start tinkering with your chair like an incompetent chair mechanic. While seated, lower it and raise it as far as it will go. Spin around in circles while you discuss the office lamprey's troubled love life. Roll around in your office chair and "test the wheels for traction" with attempts to jump over pens, binder clips, and other office supplies. While sympathetically nodding (be careful not to make eye contact), acknowledging your colleague's lonely plight, stand up from your chair and adjust the tilt levels. After each adjustment, sit back in the chair and then shake your head disapprovingly while interrupting the office lamprey's soliloquy with the statement, "Nope. At that angle I feel like I'm sitting in the space shuttle." Continue sitting and standing and making adjustments until the unwelcome visitor decides you're not worth the time.

THREE MILE ISLAND: For even the most pathological office lamprey the will to survive is greater than the need to annoy, cannibalize, and bore people. So when all other attempts to repel office lampreys fail, you can resort to the Three Mile Island approach. This entails pretending to have every illness known to humankind, thus making yourself "radioactive." Begin by messing up your hair. Place crumpled tissues all over your desk and a few on the floor. Scatter various medicine bottles throughout your cubicle. Have a picture of the Elephant Man clearly displayed on your computer screen. Fake-cough and blow your nose repeatedly. Squint as if you are in pain. Croak hoarsely as you say, "I don't know what I have. All I know is that it's not normal like a cold or fever. It's more like an avian-flu-meets-SARS

Never feed office lampreys or unwanted cubicle visitors. Don't offer them a mini Nestlé Crunch from your bowl of candy. Don't give them Starburst from your desk drawer. Like stray cats, they will associate you and your cubicle with generosity and a free meal. They will continue visiting and bothering you until you feed them again, treating you with disdain if you try to wean them off your charity. Do not feed the animals.

type of thing. What was that you wanted?" Begin to shiver if they don't go away. If none of this works, explain that your feet feel numb, you have a ringing in your ears, and you can't use your hands. Then ask them to pick up one of the crumpled tissues and hold it to your nose so you can clear your nostrils.

On Being Social and Neighborly

As a member of the cubicle community you have basic human needs and obligations that must be addressed. Most cubicle dwellers spend at least forty hours a week in their cubicles—more time than they spend with their spouses, significant others, children, and even themselves. The most effective means of combating corporate homogenization, workplace aggression, fatigue, isolation, depression, and spiritual claustrophobia is to connect with other human beings. Be sure to always think and act like a professional; but also ensure that you make friends and build collegial, perhaps personal (but not too personal, *ahem*), relationships with your colleagues. Gain the trust of those who surround you; prove that you are trustworthy. Becoming socially isolated in the workplace can lead to personal and professional ruin. Human beings are often at their worst when they function as a pack, because they frequently focus their negative energy on minorities or, even better, loners. James Dean remains America's most heralded loner with his drag races and fierce independence in *Rebel Without a Cause*. Had James Dean worked in a cubicle community, however, his independence would have been interpreted as antisocial behavior indicative of people who think they are better than everyone else. *Who does he think he is? I hear he downloads porn on his computer and masturbates in the office bathroom. Creep. He doesn't believe in the mission statement. I hope he gets fired before he brings us all down. He's dangerous. We should do something. Get him!*

If you are shy, you don't have to compromise your personality, but do make a noticeable effort to come out of your shell. If you are simply a miserable person who never feels like being friendly, chances are your employment status is tenuous at best. If you are suffering from some psychological infirmity or other disability that prevents you from being able to socialize "normally," then look into getting professional help outside your workplace. Most health care plans cover psychological treatment, and let's face it, succeeding in the corporate and cubicle environment is largely a psychological endeavor.

What can you do if being outgoing is not in your nature? Well, plenty. First of all, if you can't be welcoming, make your cubicle welcoming. Decorate your space with bright, welcoming colors that convey warmth and comfort. Display pictures of your family or other items representative of your personality, hobbies, and affiliations. Personal decorations lead to ingenuous conversations. Flip back to chapter 2 to reference specifics on how, and how not, to decorate your cubicle. Next, focus on yourself.

Sociability Positioning Techniques

You don't have to wear provocative clothes, slouch in your chair, and spread your legs like a prostitute to let your colleagues know you are interested in getting to know the people around you. You also don't have to beseech them, impress them, or act like someone you're not. You're no longer in high school. Though the adult cubicle community will invariably have cliques, annoying rules, and fire drills, it is different from the social institutions we experienced as children and young adults. The cubicle community is about one thing: the corporation. So don't worry about being the handsome quarterback, the pretty homecoming queen, or the class clown. By the time most people end up in a cubicles, life has taught them not only who they are, but how ridiculous they look when trying to be anything else. Sometimes people just need a little opening up. Following are some interaction methods that express willingness for fellowship and encourage communication.

PEN GRENADE TOSS: Whenever you overhear a compelling conversation that you wish to be included in, the Pen Grenade Toss is an effective technique for inserting yourself into the dialogue. The Pen Grenade Toss requires a deft touch, hand–eye coordination, and accuracy, so you may want to practice a few times when no one is looking. The trick is to toss your pen as if it's a hand grenade so that it simultaneously surprises and confuses the target. Simply throwing it near the conversing employees will look like a poorly orchestrated effort to ambush the conversation. However, a pen carefully lobbed or rolled into the area with an audible "oops" or "shoot" is a good cover for becoming part of the conversational environment. Make sure the cap is removed, and—if you wish to add a flair of the dramatic—have the pen cap in your hand and grimace at it as you enter the conversational area. Then quip to your colleagues, "Anyone see a pen?" Pick up the pen, put the cap on it, and say, "I think that's a sign I need a break. So what's going on with you folks?"

NON-SEQUITUR SMILE: Often the difference between people who date television stars and people who date television shows has nothing to do with appearances, intelligence, or money. The difference is that some people know how to flirt and others don't. Flirtation does not necessarily have to be a sexual thing. It can be used, and in the cubicle community should be used, as a means of expressing respect or interest. When prudent, employ body language to convey your professional thoughts and feelings. The Non-Sequitur Smile is an effective means of expressing admiration, gratitude, or general approval and interest. Do not accompany your Non-Sequitur Smile with a seductive lowering of the head, batting of the eyelashes, or roll of the tongue over your teeth. Those are seen as sexual overtures that, in the workplace, can also be viewed as sexual harassment. (The difference is apparent but should be mentioned nevertheless.)

Suppose your boss's boss doesn't know your name but makes a surprise visit to your cubicle street. You've never met her, but you want her to acknowledge your existence and hopefully make the connection that you deserve credit for the success with the Unity merger. So business-flirt. But do so without acting as if you're seeking attention, putting yourself ahead of your colleagues, or stepping into the jurisdiction of your own boss. The best way to do this is to anticipate when the boss's boss is about to walk past your cubicle, and, when she does, turn in your seat, make eye contact—make some sort of noise to get her attention if you have to—and offer a Non-Sequitur Smile. Make sure it's not too big to intimidate and seem threatening, and not so small as to go unnoticed. It should be a forceful, open smile that conveys more than mere cordiality but less than *long-lost college buddy*. The smile, though out of context, should make the recipient think, *That person seems very happy to be at work. I wonder if he was expecting me to talk to him. Was he connected to the Unity merger? I should find out who that is.* Be prepared if someone answers your smile with an introduction or friendly comment. Offering the Non-Sequitur Smile and then swiveling back around or retreating into silence will only cloud your intentions and open your reputation to all sorts of speculation. Be prepared.

Always know something personal about your boss's boss or other higher-ups. When the brass circulate through the cubicle community, they do so with apprehension and trepidation. Though they may not show it, they're worried about appearing condescending and disconnected from the nine-to-five employees. If they are good bosses, help them keep it real. When good higher-ups come unexpectedly wandering down your cubicle street, they will always remember and appreciate you if you say something like, "Sorry to hear about your Redskins, Mr. Manson." Or "Mrs. Murdock, have you tried that new Japanese place on Pushkin Avenue? I know you love sushi." Be interested without being obsequious. Insincere banter is unproductive. Deal makers hate it; nice people can smell it a mile away.

POLLINATING CLOTHES: In the animal, plant, and insect kingdoms success is often achieved through colors, patterns, and designs. Grasshoppers have tough greenish exoskeletons that protect them from the elements and help them blend into the environment. Poison oak has a three-leaf pattern that deceptively changes color when the seasons change. Blowfish are armored in a prickly, spiny brown-and-white skin that inflates when they feel threatened. At the office, however, don't dress like a grasshopper, poison oak, or a blowfish. Don't blend into the drab anonymity of your cubicle environment. Don't be defensive. Wear something outgoing and friendly, yet professional. Dress like a colorful butterfly, an elegant orchid, or the dapper goldring surgeonfish. The rules of the great outdoors also apply in the cubicle community: How you look says a lot about you. Cubicles offer little room for self-expression, so embellish the aesthetics of your cubicle by improving yourself.

HANDS-ON ATTRACTIONS: Okay, so you're shy, and so are your clothes. You don't like hanging pictures of your family on your cubicle walls, and every time you touch a plant it droops like a twelve-year-old without a PlayStation. What can you do to attract colleagues to your cubicle? Provide Hands-On Attractions. It's astonishing how many cubicle people want to know what the ambient humidity is. Or the temperature. Or that same

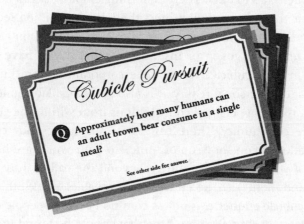

Cubicle Pursuit

Q Approximately how many humans can an adult brown bear consume in a single meal?

See other side for answer.

temperature in centigrade. Small combination hygrometers-thermometers that perfectly augment a cubicle environment are widely available, and they render their owners the popular role of local meteorologist in the cubicle neighborhood. Whenever someone says, "Are you cold? It feels cold in here" or "Am I the only one burning up in here?" a colleague will answer, "Ask the shy new programmer in 4-A. The girl dressed like a hospital curtain. She has a contraption on her desk that tells the temperature *and* humidity." If the interior atmospheric conditions don't interest you, find a Hands-On Attraction that bridges your and your colleagues' interests. Perhaps a chart of zodiac signs that offers alignment configurations and horoscope interpretations. Or maybe something as simple as a small dry-erase board where you can post your own "Quote of the Day." Just refrain from using any Hands-On Attractions that make noises, are expensive, or are time consuming. Sure, bring the box of Trivial Pursuit questions, but leave the game board at home.

WORK ETHIC: If office interactions make you feel as if you are being stoned by a mob of self-righteous zealots, a Work Ethic can protect you from any threat or assault the cubicle environment has to offer. There is nothing employees can do to or in their cubicles that will protect their reputation, job security, and general happiness as much as a Work Ethic. Don't worry about the local gossip or insidious rumors if you have Work Ethic in your cubicle. Though the corporate bottom line is a crass and impersonal reality, it is also an unassailable guideline when assessing personal contributions from within the general cubicle community. There can be no disputing your cubicle reputation if you show up on time, do your work, are honest, control your downtime, and go beyond the call of duty every now and then. Also, be efficient and reliable. Work Ethic, like good cubicle etiquette, is not as common as most people think. This basic attribute is something that should be found in every cubicle, but isn't. If you have Work Ethic, you will enjoy plenty of respectful and constructive visits from your colleagues.

Quick Quiz Self-Assessment

(1) Identify which trait(s) is *not* characteristic of office lampreys:
  (a) Feed parasitically.
  (b) Wear trendy clothes.
  (c) Ingratiate themselves with host before attaching.
  (d) Bleed life out of host with endless, boring stories and anecdotes.

(e) Feed off host until it is dead.

(f) Is named for a snail-like creature that lives in Caribbean coral reefs.

(2) True or False? The Cold War Dip is an evasive cubicle body-language and positioning technique named for the USS *Alexandria*, a Cold War–era nuclear-powered submarine that reached a depth of 3,740 feet in the Arctic Ocean while intercepting messages from international telecom cables resting on the seafloor. Today it refers to lying low under your desk, thereby avoiding detection from passing office lampreys and other cubicle community threats.

(3) While in Photoshop's "Brushstrokes" option in the "Filter" dropdown menu, Doug Barbour decided to go with "Spatter" to give a diaphanous look to the latest newsletter for the National Association of Atmospheric Studies. Actually, he made that decision three hours ago, and has spent most of the afternoon thinking of ways to break up with Jenna, his girlfriend. For that task he decided to go with the "Act Like a Jerk Until She Breaks Up with Me" option in the "I Lied When I Said I Loved You" menu. They really were, after all, just one of those couples who hook up after several drinks. Suddenly Doug overhears people talking by the plastic palm tree with fabric green fronds. It's Jackson Bugel from IT and Jennifer Coley from marketing. They're discussing putting together an impromptu happy hour for that night. Doug wants to be invited. Jennifer Coley, after all, was recently dumped by her lawyer boyfriend and, according to cubicle community gossip, "has had it with the over-educated, teased-hair-with-gel types." Without appearing obvious, which of the following communication techniques should Doug employ to become part of the conversation and get himself invited to the happy hour?

(a) Pen Grenade Toss

(b) Hands-On Attractions

(c) Greek Shoulder Block

(d) Work Ethic

(e) Pollinating Clothes

(f) Roller-Coaster Neck Suplex

(g) Non-Sequitur Smile

(h) Ammonia Cloud Blink

ANSWERS:

(1) b. Office lampreys are known for wearing clothes that neither fit nor match. e. Killing the host would get office lampreys in serious trouble, so they suck the life out of the host until it is near death, but never until dead. f. The office lamprey is named for an eel-like parasite that uses sharp teeth and anticoagulants to feed off a host.

(2) False. the Cold War Dip is a defensive body-language and positioning technique named for a survival skill taught to millions of American and Russian schoolchildren during the Cold War. The maneuver involves scrambling out of your chair and under your desk, then placing your head between your knees and locking your hands over the back of your head. Then crapping your pants. Today this defensive cubicle strategy is also known as the A-Bomb Duck or, in many earthquake-prone areas such as Japan, the Earthquake Drop.

(3) a. The Pen Grenade Toss. Doug's best chance of gracefully inserting himself into the conversation and getting invited to the happy hour is by murmuring "Oops" and lobbing his black felt-tip pen into the corridor behind his cubicle, toward the fake palm tree. With the pen top in hand and perhaps a few black pen marks on his hand, Doug should say, "Sheesh. You know you're at the end of your rope when your pen doesn't want to cooperate. I could use a beer."

CHAPTER EIGHT

Anti-Spy Methods and Counterespionage Equipment

t its essence human dignity is about respect, and respect is about trust. Your employers say they trust you; that's why they hired you. That's what interviews are for—they're the company's effort to fill jobs with qualified, trustworthy people. If the corporation didn't trust you, you'd be working somewhere else, or not at all. Yet corporate policy dictates that all computer monitors must face the missing fourth wall. Why? Because they want to see what you are doing. Don't get upset; you agreed to take the job. Furthermore, computers, phones, and all other office equipment is owned by the company and not to be used for personal purposes. Why? Because the company is protecting its own interests, supposedly maximizing productivity by minimizing employees' inclination to focus on their personal affairs. Distractions are bad for the bottom line. So your employers monitor your e-mail activity. They catalog the websites you visit. They prohibit you from using company resources to, say, write a book about cubicle survival.

Is this fair? Yes, it is. But it's nothing personal; it's business.

A company that doesn't care about productivity and the bottom line is a company that won't successfully employ many people for very long. The truth is, corporations don't trust individual employees because corporations don't deal with individual employees. The corporation sees a workforce, which you are part of. The corporation makes rules according to human nature, not according to human beings. So don't be offended. Accept this reality or find a new career. Seriously.

For some reason, like alcoholics and drug addicts, disgruntled employees lose perspective on their lives and often have to hit rock bottom before they see things for how they really are. Don't be one of these people. There is no shame in admitting you're not fit for the cubicle lifestyle. Countless people have gotten themselves fired by not being able to accept this reality. Truthfully, all the education, advice, and training in the world does little to prepare people for cubicle life. Understanding how to survive in a cubicle is a philosophical endeavor that requires perspective, discipline, and—contrary to pop-culture mythology—plenty of self-esteem. Neophyte actors and prima donnas with dreams of fame and superficial riches should not work in cubicles; they should wait tables, as they have since the beginning of time. In the cubicle community, all those who need to prove to the rest of the world how beautiful and gifted they are will be eaten by fellow employees like a leftover pizza in the office kitchen.

Generally, cubicle dwellers know who they are, where they belong, and what they stand for. That's why it's so imperative to understand the unspoken rules and expectations of life in the cubicle community. It can be an unforgiving environment for everyone from recent college graduates working their way up the corporate ladder to seasoned veterans sliding into cynicism and apathy. Don't let the men's manicured eyebrows and the women's lotioned hands fool you: Cubicle life is tough, and so are cubicle people. They have to be.

Being part of the grueling corporate machine requires fortitude. Cubicle dwellers do not break because they find strength in their family lives, faith or spirituality, senses of humor, or remarkable hobbies—or they're simply mature enough to understand that life is difficult, ephemeral, and, in the long run, often anonymous. They do not harbor any complexes or insecurities about being nameless Employee #0090037050. Cubicle dwellers understand the big picture. Deep down, they know that Alpha Centauri is 4.35 light-years away from our sun. They know that *Tyrannosaurus rex* was the fiercest dinosaur during the Cretaceous period about eighty-five to sixty-five million years ago. They know not to get drunk at the office holiday party (who cares, corporate moved it to a Sunday afternoon, anyway). They know that for the sake of efficiency, corporations have stripped cubicle communities of privacy, individuality, and, in the process, dignity. They know that in order to survive, in order to preserve the uniqueness of their souls, they must fight the corporation on its own turf—and they must win.

Though the company says it trusts you, and upon accepting the position you imply that you trust it, never for a moment be lulled into a false sense of security. The company benefits by making you work as much as possible for as little compensation as possible. Cubicle dwellers benefit by working not as little as possible, but as much as they deem is fair and not a second more. The feeling of being exploited leads to bad habits, low self-esteem, and an early death with lots of medical bills. The corporation won't even chip in for your coffin. Rarely do corporate and the cubicle dweller agree on what the latter's time is worth. But remember, as in gambling, the house always wins. In a capitalistic society, the house is the corporation, and its rooms have four walls, real plants, large wooden desks, and CEOs who learned how to sail in grade school. So look out for number one.

The daily grind of real cubicle life is a battle between

corporate policy and human will. Give yourself a fighting chance, or else suffocate in the plastic bag of company policy. Purchasing this book is an excellent start in protecting your personal interests and identity. Now you just have to follow through. Do it for your children—that is, if you love them.

The Resistance Arsenal

Below are some popular methods cubicle dwellers have developed to resist corporate attempts to coerce human employees into acting like soulless machines. Use these tactics wisely and cautiously. They are most effective when used in tandem, and only after you've studied your work environment and established a clear strategy. Experiment with these methods and combinations of them so that a maximum level of protection exists between you, your cubicle, and corporate efforts to document your actions, judge your intentions, and control your behavior.

MINIMIZE QUICK CLICK: Nothing has done more to improve America's hand–eye coordination than the Minimize Quick Click. Who knew that back in the 1980s, the Atari 1200 was basic training for an American workforce that would use video-game skills not to combat descending missiles or space aliens, but corporate domination? Fortunately, today the Play-Station and Xbox have picked up where Atari left off, and training for America's future cubicle dwellers continues. Despite all the negative things that are said about video games, such as that they encourage violence and a sedentary lifestyle, they do prepare our nation's young people for a professional life spent in front of a computer. Indeed, most people who work in a cubicle community can "X" out of The Drudge Report, espn.com, or the Williams-Sonoma home page faster than they can blink.

The Minimize Quick Click has been around since the dawn of the Internet and entails closing a webpage displayed on your monitor by clicking the "_" in the upper right-hand corner. Or the "F11" key for you Mac users. The displayed webpage is minimized before anyone notices that you have been watching your stock portfolio instead of performing your assigned workplace duties.

There are variations on the traditional Minimize Quick Click, which just about any veteran cubicle dweller is already familiar with. For instance, the Overcrowded Task Manager Bar is a common modification of the Minimize Quick Click. The Overcrowded Task Manager Bar entails opening several or more browsers and other software applications so that the task manager bar becomes so crowded with applications that it is impossible to tell exactly what responsibilities a particular employee is working on.

"CTRL" "W": Before the mouse, that little pencil eraser nodule thing, and the touch pad, the only way computer users interacted with their computer screens was through the keyboard or by picking up the monitor and throwing it at the wall. Even though technology advances at an almost blinding speed, there are a few tricks that remain relevant today, if not vital. The "ctrl" "w" technique is one of them. It's a legacy stealth tactic. With proper training, you can quickly hit the "ctrl" button and then "w" to instantly close the program currently on your screen. Mac users can perform this maneuver by hitting "apple" and "w." This is a surreptitious way to exit programs when you hear a potential human threat approaching your cubicle. This technique is acoustically invisible in that it does not emit the widely recognized panic click of the mouse. In addition, many people don't know that this option even exists. So for its speed, covertness, and general effectiveness, the "ctrl" "w" is a highly recommended means of clearing your screen. It takes little time to master and is a reliable tool in protecting your privacy on the job.

POKER SCREEN SHUFFLE: Any card player will tell you that the first skill you need to learn is to hold your cards so that other people cannot see them. If other players at the table are able to discern what you are holding, they also have insight into what you are thinking, which gives them the keys to unlocking your behavior, intentions, offenses, defenses, and general truthfulness. In essence, they know everything about you. And it's your fault.

The same principle applies in your cubicle when you are shopping online, surfing the Web, e-mailing friends, writing the great American novel, or checking the weather. No one should see what cards you are holding. Especially people who could use that information against you. Hold your webpages and open software programs so no one can see them. Use the Poker Screen Shuffle. Click the middle box in the upper left corner, the one between the complete minimize function and the "X" that closes the window. This will reduce your window so that its dimensions are reduced by about half, making it easy to slide the open program around your computer screen. Including all the way to the bottom, where you can hide it. This is the software equivalent of laying cards facedown on the table—although it's actually even better, because you can arrange them so that no one knows how many you have. Like cards, you can stack the programs or layer them on top of one another. If you forget which program is where in the stack, simply click on the task manager bar and the respective program will appear on top, with only the informative title bar visible. Even if the program pops up, it isn't visible because it doesn't rise above the task bar level. If you need to take a peek, click on the title bar and slowly drag the program into view until you see what you need to see. Mac users, unfortunately, are not provided this advantage. Mac users can use the "F10" button to reduce window dimensions, but should remember they can't move the windows. If you would like to manipulate the web-page or program by clicking or writing, simply continue to drag it from the bottom of the monitor screen until the desired work area is accessible. By using the Poker Screen Shuffle technique, cubicle dwellers should be able to effectively and covertly work on personal projects throughout their entire workday.

Suppose, for example, that Trent Humes is working on a PowerPoint presentation about his company's latest break-through in chemical polymers and durable plastic technology. Suddenly Trent receives an e-mail from his responsible daughter reminding him that his wedding anniversary is in two weeks. If he forgets, like he did last year, his daughter explains, "Mom will probably leave you. I don't blame her. And just to let you know, if she does leave, I'll be staying with her this summer until it's time to go back to college. Honestly, Dad. Get it together." Trent quickly closes the e-mail, and his boss appears from behind him like one of the creatures from the movie *Alien* (or *Aliens*, but not the disappointing *Aliens 3*, where you actually rooted for the creatures to kill the human beings).

"How's that PowerPoint presentation coming along?" Trent's boss asks, leaning over Trent's shoulder and scanning his computer screen for signs of goofing around.

"Fine," he says. "Great."

His boss steps back, knowing he has done what he gets paid to do. "Good to hear," he says. "Good to hear."

Trent turns and gives his boss a dispassionate *you can leave now* expression. "Yep," he says, "it's all good."

"Good to hear," the boss says, and walks off.

Trent immediately embarks on a search for bed-and-breakfast

joints in his area. Since his boss is lurking around, he'll have to go stealth. The first step is to camouflage his search by using the Overcrowded Task Manager Bar version of the Minimize Quick Click. In addition to PowerPoint and e-mail, he opens three browsers and Microsoft Word. He leaves Photoshop closed because it slows down his computer too much, but he does decide to open Microsoft Excel and Microsoft Access. His task manager bar is crowded to the point that no one can actually read the names of the open applications. Only the icons and "Microso" can be seen on the task bar. Trent looks busy and legit.

The next step is to search on his opened browsers for webpages related to his PowerPoint presentation just in case he clicks on one in a panic. He types in "polymer news" and "plastic revolution"—but, on the last browser, he types "bed breakfast Chesapeake Bay." He researches frantically, hoping he can not only find a bed-and-breakfast not completely booked for the weekend after next, but one that books reservations online as well. This way he doesn't have to do it over his office phone or leave his cubicle. Trent spends thirty-five minutes conducting his search until he finds Town & Glory Bed & Breakfast: Bayside Views of Rural Virginia. He decides not to mention to his wife the nearby Civil War battlefields they will certainly visit. He retrieves his credit card and begins making reservations online. Suddenly his boss approaches, talking with Derrick Stevens about the upcoming presentation. He points his cursor on the task manager bar and quickly clicks. The Town & Glory Bed & Breakfast website disappears behind a blank Excel spreadsheet.

"And here's the man with all the answers," his boss says, leading Derrick Stevens into Trent's cubicle.

"How long will this presentation . . . Why are you using Excel? I thought we decided no spreadsheets. They bore people. That's how we lost the MicroScience contract."

"Ah, I was . . ." Trent clicks blindly only to realize disaster has fallen upon him. *Bing! Bing! Bing!* rings from his computer speakers. He can't close Excel. He should be staring at a webpage about polymers or PowerPoint or his e-mail, but for some reason he's trapped. Trent's boss and Derrick Stevens quizzically look at each other.

"Is there a problem?" the boss asks.

Trent realizes what the problem is. The most universally and intensely hated computer personality known to humankind has invaded his computer screen, and they are staring at each other eye-to-eye: the freaking Office Assistant Paperclip. Where did he come from? Trent thought he was dead. Trent attacks him with his cursor and clicks all over him as if he's firing an AK-47. The Paperclip *bings* back at Trent. He's killing Trent. He's impenetrable. Trent can't get rid of him. Trent can't close out of Excel. Trent's boss is embarrassed, and Derrick Stevens, who barely knows Trent, is beginning to think he is a moron. That's what he'll tell his colleagues over in product development.

Trent takes a deep breath and remembers that being ambushed by the Office Assistant Paperclip is like drowning in a dam; the trick is not to panic. He closes his eyes and blocks out his boss, Derrick Stevens, and the presentation. Trent envisions killing the Office Assistant Paperclip. He imagines the Paperclip's soul and hunts for its weaknesses. Trent remembers to open him up and kill him from the inside. Trent clicks the Paperclip open and goes for the heart. Direct hit. The Paperclip winks insidiously and disappears (surely to fight again another day). Trent right-clicks and closes his Internet browsers. The day has been saved. Trent brings up PowerPoint and coolly rotates in his swivel chair so that he faces his boss and Derrick Stevens.

"That depends," Trent says. "If we give them the hard sell, it might take up to an hour. And no, we're not using any spreadsheets. I just use Excel to crunch numbers sometimes. And according to those numbers it's going to be hard to turn down our services."

"Good to hear," his boss says. "Let's run across the street for a cup of coffee and talk about the itinerary. We'll fly out to Chicago together weekend after next."

"Works for me," Derrick Stevens says.

"I thought I had something planned. Anyway, if it's important it'll come back to me," Trent says. "Windy City, here we come."

Three weeks later Trent receives the divorce papers in the mail. The Office Assistant Paperclip laughs from deep within Trent's hard drive. Another one bites the dust.

Of course, the lesson to be learned from the previous anecdote is to be organized. No one ever achieved stealth by winging it. Be prepared, careful, and well practiced.

CUBE TIP

The dreaded Office Assistant Paperclip who claims "my job is to help you with this application" is neither helpful nor a real paper clip. No matter how tempting it is to try to click it to death, the Office Assistant Paperclip is impervious to your assault. Take time to read the options and *then* go for the kill.

When done correctly, Minimize Quick Click is an instantaneous and instinctual action. It's lightning-fast and can only be seen on film in slow motion, like that Discovery Channel footage of the chameleon snagging a grasshopper with its sticky tongue. Zap. All the Minimize Quick Click takes is a rapid twitch of the index finger on your mouse and you're covered—working hard. Of course, it takes more than mechanical training and muscle memory for the Minimize Quick Click to work effectively. Special forces in the military know that it takes more than weaponry and a few skills to be successful. The difference between life and death behind enemy lines and in a corporate setting is often a matter of mental stamina, focus, and intellectual alacrity. Focus on the mission in front of you but know who is watching you and how. Memorize patterns and routines.

Study Your Environment

We've all seen those movies where inmates break out of jails, prisons, and POW camps. Whether the escape is from a rural county jail, Alcatraz Island, or a World War II German prisoner-of-war facility, all of the strategies share a common tactic: The escapees memorize the patterns and routines of the guards and the security system. In the sometimes prison-like conditions of the cubicle community, these same measures should be utilized as you seek freedom from the oppressive corporate environment. Avoid the spotlight that accusingly drifts over the landscape of your cubicle community. Learn the patterns of your capturers, whether they are meddling bosses, tattletale colleagues, or saboteur co-workers who want you to look bad for their own professional gain. Know when your bosses and colleagues take their coffee breaks, go to lunch, visit the watercooler, use the fax machine, and take any other excursion that will bring them past your cubicle and within sight of your monitor. Don't think for a minute that passersby don't care what's on your computer screen. It's human nature to see if people are working and playing by the rules. Know that Sheila Smithson, two cubes down, takes her purse everywhere, and you can usually hear her keys jingle as she walks. Listen for nosy Rich Develli, who always plays with the change in his pocket as he nervously walks around the cubicle community soliciting gossip. Cynthia Grant's chair gently squeaks before she gets out of it and passes your cubicle on the way to the bathroom. Donald Henry snorts no matter where he is or what he's doing. A cool draft scurries around your ankles whenever clients are brought through the front door and past your cubicle on the way to the conference room.

Make maps in your mind. Look for signs of activity. Listen for movement. Be aware of what is going on around you. Train your senses to stay active, particularly when you read online newspapers, book flights, trade stocks, e-mail friends, buy camping gear, or participate in message boards while at work. Being a professional in the cubicle community often means looking like a professional more than acting like one.

Make Alliances

Though many corporations try to persuade employees that they are part of a "family," most cubicle inhabitants don't fall for this propaganda because it is okay to drink beer, hug, and fight with your family members. Any of those actions in the modern workplace would get the employee fired, arrested, or both. For the most part, any company that attempts to convince employees that they are part of a family does not respect its employees. In essence, it thinks its employees are stupid enough to go the extra mile because a spirited human resource representative and a few motivational posters will convince them that CEOs scuba diving in the Cayman Islands love employees as much as their own grandmothers.

The "family" analogy is a shining example of the crass cynicism and condescension too often found in the corporate environment. It doesn't make people feel loved. It makes them feel trapped in a sci-fi netherworld where omnipotent international corporations do not employ people but raise them in antiseptic laboratories, feeding them from vending machines and teaching them that they're part of a so-called family that has its own flags, coffee mugs, T-shirts, and fleece pullovers. All of which, of course, glorify the company logo. Chairman Mao, Adolf Hitler, and Pol Pot used similar tactics to garner loyalty in their business ventures—political persecution, ethnic cleansing, and violent oppression.

Thankfully, rebellion is also part of human nature, and rebellions require solidarity. So find colleagues with whom you share common interests and gain their trust. Become friends with co-workers and establish sincere, positive relationships. Let the people you trust know they can trust you. Be dependable and don't act like you're on one of those ridiculous reality shows. In reality, no one who can catch his own fish would leave a tropical paradise to go back to installing drywall.

Over time, quite naturally, you and the members of your alliance will begin looking after one another and develop a complicated and vital communication network. By depending on one another you can pass on important information about corporate restructuring, firings, opening job advancement opportunities, or gossip such as why the receptionist was crying in the stairwell. The book and movie *Black Hawk Down* taught us that penniless kids burning car tires on the outskirts of Mogadishu can warn their compatriots in plenty of time about US troops advancing in million-dollar helicopters. Imagine how well you can insulate yourself by having your own compatriots spread throughout the company armed with telephones, e-mail, and instant messages. With a proper alliance in place, you should never be surprised by the arrival of an unwanted presence. (If this does happen, immediately establish your next line of defense by consulting chapter 7.)

Set up redundant and fail-safe lines of communication so that multiple members of your alliance can warn one another when threats arise. Like when macho David Molson and his yellow teeth are on their way to flirt with pretty alliance member Angela Samuels. Or when the angry boss who needs to blame someone other than herself for not dropping off the overnight packages is heading over to low-self-esteem alliance member Kyle O'Malley. Or when office lamprey Sean Lee is making a beeline over to alliance member Megan Springer, who was featured in the metro section of today's newspaper for her nineteenth-century-Balkan ceramic doll collection. The fundamental rule of alliance correspondence is never to assume someone else is taking care of it. Be on top of the situation and call, e-mail, or message an alliance member who is in imminent danger of being ambushed by an annoying colleague, irate boss, or sex-deprived co-worker looking for attention. Meet regularly and exchange information regarding your workplace.

But always remember that your computer belongs to the corporation. Everything you say via e-mail, website, or instant message is open to corporate scrutiny and admissible evidence in the crusade against rebellious individuals and freethinking alliances. Remember: Corporate is always watching you.

Cover Electronic Footprints

Despite copious experience, education, and intelligence, there are always members of the cubicle community who convince themselves that no one is watching their behavior on the computer. After all, government officials should be more concerned with chasing terrorists and international cyber criminals, while corporate IT employees are always busy fighting viruses, spyware, spam, and hackers. Who is left to monitor individual employee behavior other than the individual employees? Answer: fans of *The Matrix*, hardworking employees with accents and H-1B visas, the pale corpse about whom you once quipped "Should hit the beach," and nearly anyone with a key to the server room. No matter how isolated you may feel, on the Internet you are never alone or anonymous. Visiting a forbidden website on the company computer is like murdering a giraffe in Antarctica. You may be able to get away with it, but it's pretty easy to trace your bloody footprints back to the scene of the crime. For better or for worse, human beings are flawed and we all have our vices, shortcomings, weaknesses, and vulnerabilities to particular temptations. Especially when we're bored—at work, for example.

Cyberspace is the next great frontier, and when human beings begin planting stakes in that frontier and trying to profit from it, rest assured that every step into it will be recorded, time-stamped, and cataloged for some overpriced marketing firm to analyze. It is only a matter of time before corporations fill cyberspace with strip malls, amusement parks, surcharges, afflictions, online cures for those afflictions, and the latest trends in superficiality. With a valid credit card, you can have everything cyberspace has to offer. Including your own electronic profile and cyberspace travel history. Welcome to the information age, where you can be known to millions but still remain lonely, depressed, isolated, and unfulfilled. It's like being a movie star.

There are, thankfully, several precautions cubicle inhabitants can take to better cloak their identities and erase their electronic footprints. First, familiarize yourself with "Internet Options."

COOKIES: If you have ever seen the movie *Total Recall* and watched Arnold Schwarzenegger pull that glowing red ball out of his nose, then you know what a cookie is. A cookie is a tracking device that webservers shove up your nasal passage as thanks for visiting their home pages. Technically, a cookie is a small text file that attaches to your computer's hard drive. It's basically innocuous and cannot transmit viruses or crash your computer. What makes cookies a blessing and a curse, however, is that they enable the websites you visit to remember who you are. If you want Amazon.com to remember that you bought *How to Make Your Own Yarn* and the sadly ironic novel by Frida Juarez, *Love Is a Watered Lily*, then you probably think cookies are great. The next time you visit Amazon.com, they will even remember your name and suggest recommendations based on your past purchases. If you don't have many friends, these hollow gestures can be quite fulfilling. If, on the other hand, you purchased *How to Grow Your Own Pot in Your Neighbor's Yard* and the sublimely ironic novel by Rodney Hawkson, *Nowhere Is Everywhere*, then you might be inclined to remain anonymous. It is up to individual cubicle inhabitants to decide if, and which, cookies they wish to have on their hard drive. As a general rule, corporate frowns upon cookies with "XXX" or "sex" or "moneyshot" as part of their text. For pathological employees who can't resist visiting dubious websites, there is always the option of adjusting the privacy settings to "High" so that most, or all, cookies are blocked from the hard drive.

DELETE HISTORY: If you have seen the movie *Eternal Sunshine of the Spotless Mind* and understood why Jim Carrey would visit the beach in the dead of winter, then you know what "Delete History" means. "Delete History" does to your Internet navigation past what many of us wish we could do to our own pasts. "Delete History" erases your computer's memories of life on the Web. It wipes the slate clean—no regrets, no guilt, none of the remorse. It's the cyberspace equivalent to being born again. However, as Jim Carrey discovers in *Eternal Sunshine*, deleting memories is a double-edged sword because in the process we lose part of who we are. We sacrifice our identity for a new beginning, which is complicated in movies, religion, and technology. By clicking on "Delete History" your online newspaper will not recognize you and will treat you like a stranger. It will be as if you are visiting the site for the first time, and therefore must input your user ID and password to be given access. Your favorite message boards won't remember your past visits, either. You will have to re-register with your online shopping vendors as if you had never existed before. The drop-down menu on your browser will be startlingly empty. If these things don't bother you, then use your "Delete History" function at work to eliminate your computer's record of your cyber travels. Besides, nothing feels better than new beginnings and the opportunity to make history, and the same mistakes, all over again.

TEMPORARY FILES OR CACHE: People, including cubicle inhabitants, are creatures of habit, and no one capitalizes on this truth more than marketers and web developers. Via the temporary file or cache—which is basically an information-storage mechanism allowing quick access to frequently utilized material—companies observe customers' routines, desires, fears, and patterns of behavior. You have probably reasoned that it's safer to use your personal e-mail account rather than your work e-mail at the office. Good thinking. Personal lives are best discussed on personal e-mail accounts. (But remember that your computer is still company property and you are not entitled to privacy or even a glance in the other direction by company watchdogs. So be good.) If you decided to clear your temporary files or cache, remember that your personal e-mail Web-based viewer information is stored on your work computer. You will lose your personal e-mail settings, along with your customized weather, sports, and news resources. Though you may lose the convenience of being recognized and feeling popular, you gain the security of not having a reputation. That anonymity, in addition to recovered disk space, will probably make you a better-protected and more efficient employee.

Use a Small Font

Once you have mastered the art of minimizing and camouflaging open programs, you are ready to fine-tune your stealth activities. With any type of correspondence or writing—from your e-mail to the book you're writing about cubicle survival at work using Microsoft Word—minimize the screen and change the font size so that passersby cannot read your words. Most co-workers who stop by your cubicle for either professional or personal reasons can read Times New Roman font size 12 from six feet away. However, if you are writing in font size 10 or smaller, chances are they can't read what you're writing. They need to be almost as close to your computer screen as you are, thus allowing you plenty of time to either minimize or close your correspondence before anyone has the opportunity to read it. If you're composing an involved e-mail on a personal Web-based account, it's best to write it in software such as Microsoft Word so that you can save it and not worry about timing out.

Bury Your Personal Files and Folders

Your computer desktop says a lot about you. What you have buried deep within the icons on that desktop says even more. That is, assuming you are saving and storing your personal files and folders like a professional. Savvy cubicle dwellers know to make several decoy folders on their desktops so that their personal files are both well hidden and easily accessible. For example, you might create three new folders on your desktop and name them something relevant but general such as "Client Files," "Program Development," and "Tech Regulations." When your co-workers see these folders, they will assume you are an organized and focused employee. You, however, will know that these folders contain additional folders and files that contain your personal material. The more personal the information, the deeper you bury it in your filing system. Save your twenty-three-page poem about your spurned love and emotional instability in the "Program Development" folder, then in the "Cursory Assessments" subfolder, then in the "Approval Parameters" sub-subfolder. Name the document "Improvement Calibrations." The key is to be methodical and meticulous. Saving a personal file somewhere inappropriate or downright foolish on your company's hard drive or, even worse, shared drive can result in embarrassment or termination. By keeping your personal files in the same, specific folders, you reduce the chances of losing something personal . . . only to have it found by the entire company.

Rearview Mirror

All cubicle inhabitants realize that the most vulnerable point in their defenses is their back. Sneak attacks by bosses with accusatory questions, drive-by monitor glances from nosy colleagues, predatory pounces from incompetently flirtatious admirers, and office lampreys and their sudden latchings-on are all assaults from the blind side. Fortunately, none of these people is invisible. Many employees who work in cubicles attach small mirrors to their monitors so they can see whomever, or whatever, is behind them. This is an excellent strategy.

Mirrors come in various shapes and styles. Some are more discreet than others. Some cubicle dwellers use small, makeup-kit-size mirrors; there are folks out there, surely, who have rearview mirrors from Cadillacs mounted atop their monitors to highlight the fact they are either clueless or damn funny. (It would be even funnier if it were a side mirror with OBJECTS ARE CLOSER THAN THEY APPEAR written on it.) Choose one that fits your sensibility and working environment.

Most employees realize mirrors are difficult, if not impossible, to camouflage, so they place the mirrors where they provide the clearest and widest rear perspective. Keep in mind, however, that your co-workers and bosses will learn something about you if you decide to mount a rearview mirror. They know you are in the espionage and counterespionage game. They know you are employed by the company but work for you. So be prepared to back up your boldness and explain why you believe it necessary to have a rearview mirror in your cubicle. Be politically correct, deft, and confident. The spy game is not for the slow or weak of heart. When asked if you feel as if you have something to hide, answer, "No, I feel as if I have something to protect, like the privacy of my clients and colleagues with whom I correspond. As a professional it's my business to ensure a level of trust with business associates. You never know who can come snooping along looking for trouble. Now please excuse me." Just make sure that while you're having this conversation, you never turn around.

Quick Quiz Self-Assessment

(1) It's five thirty on Thursday afternoon, and tomorrow Britney Pierson, her husband, and two children are driving to her parents' new assisted-living facility to celebrate her

mother's birthday. Her mother is turning seventy-five; it's a big one. The assisted-living facility is in Portland, Maine. Nancy lives near Cubers International, in a ranch house outside Buffalo. Her boss, Edmund, wants the Tax Ax Money Management profile edited and ready to go by six o'clock. Edmund passive-aggressively walks back and forth past Britney's cubicle, occasionally popping in to ask if she needs any help, which Britney knows he can't provide. In addition to completing the Tax Ax Money Management profile by six, Britney needs to (i) order a customized daffodil-and-tulip arrangement for morning delivery to her mother in Portland, (ii) search and print driving directions to the new retirement facility, (iii) check tomorrow's weather forecast and driving conditions, (iv) research and print out information about the Bowdoin ice hockey team for her husband to read so he'll have something to talk to her father about instead of fighting, and (v) e-mail their dog-sitter because she forgot to mention that Darby likes a dollop of wet canned food on her bowl of dry food, otherwise she won't eat it.

To accomplish all of these tasks while finishing the Tax Ax Money Management profile, Britney might use one or more of the following anti-spy, counterespionage technique(s). Rank them in order from most to least effective:

(a) "Delete History"
(b) Minimize Quick Click with Overcrowded Task Manager Bar
(c) "ctrl" "w"
(d) Bury Files
(e) Make Alliances
(f) Rearview Mirror
(g) Small Font
(h) Minimize Quick Click
(i) Poker Screen Shuffle

(2) True or False? *Cookie* is a term that was co-opted by the public relations firm ProCom, which was hired in 1989 by the American Computer Industries Association (ACIA). ProCom specializes in "surrogate vocabulary and image restructuring" and is responsible for various alternative definitions, such as replacing the word *overpriced* with *organic, ergonomic,* or *boutique.* Other ProCom coups include *surcharge* instead of *mugging,* and the phrase *Your call is important to us* in place of *Not only do we not care, but the person with whom you're about to converse can't speak English.* When the ACIA approached ProCom with the description "a small file that allows profit-obsessed corporations to invisibly monitor the spending habits of unsuspecting customers," ProCom, after six months of intense research, came up with *cookie.* ProCom's original choice of *sugar cookie* was said to be misleading.

(3) A good example of "studying your environment" would be:
  (a) Researching the deforestation of the rain forest on the Internet while putting off calling clients and responding to your boss's e-mail about recent developments in your attitude.
  (b) Using Post-it notes stuck to your monitor to document your co-workers' habits, such as the duration of their bathroom breaks, the number of occasions you believe they secretly pick their nose, or how they react every time you shout "Emergency!"
  (c) Memorizing the professional and personal patterns and dispositions of your colleagues so you can manipulate how your work ethics are perceived.
  (d) Making your own census forms and going from cubicle to cubicle asking colleagues how many people they have living in their cubicles,

and knowing that if they all answer "one," there is some sort of illegal immigration conspiracy at hand.

ANSWERS:

(1) For task (i), answer (i), the Poker Screen Shuffle. Perfect for covertly juggling several open applications.

For task (ii), answer (b), Minimize Quick Click with Overcrowded Task Manager Bar. This is also an effective tool for hiding multiple open applications.

For task (iii), answer (h), Minimize Quick Click. This popular technique is, alas, less useful when dealing with more than one application. Answer (c), "ctrl" "w," would also be correct, although this old-school tool is better for single open applications.

For task (iv), answer (e), Make Alliances. Very useful when your network of allies is aware of your objectives and in a position to stop, divert, or warn of arrival of the enemy. Answer (f), Rearview Mirror, is also appropriate. A show of confidence and force will help identify oncoming assaults but may also encourage unspoken disdain from higher-ups.

For task (v), answer (g), Small Font. This technique helps prevent prying eyes from being able to read when you're composing an e-mail or prose document, which, in this example, would help Nancy with e-mailing her dog-sitter.

For all of these tasks, answer (d) is fully apt. Burying Files is a great aid in organizing, storing, and concealing documents you've finished working on. (2) False. *Cookie* is the nickname for a glowing red ball that evil companies shove up your nose so they can track your cyber travels. (3) c. Studying your cubicle environment must be done without notice, because anything that knows it is being studied will change its behavior. For example, when regular, talentless actors realize they are being covered by the tabloids, they start acting like spoiled, talented actors and begin abusing drugs to help convince themselves they deserve the attention.

CHAPTER NINE

Exercising, Blood Circulation, and Posture

Psychological health and physical health are tightly interwoven. Americans have become so overdiagnosed and overmedicated, however, that we don't know whether to blame our suburban upbringing or our Irish Catholic genes for catching a cold. Unfortunately, cubicle communities are breeding grounds for both mental anguish and physical apathy. The best way cubicle inhabitants can defend their overall health is through disciplined physical activity and a basic medical understanding of the human condition. This chapter offers advice on both.

The difference between a flu epidemic and an obesity epidemic is that for the latter, you actually have to pay for and eat the disease. Unfortunately, both are common ailments among cubicle communities. People smart enough to be hired by corporate are also smart enough to know that corporations need money to exist, and the only way to get this money is to have people hand it to them. And the best way to compel people into giving their money away is to become a desired or necessary part of their habits and lifestyles. Make them dependent on your product. This seems harmless, but it isn't, because people, in general, are lazy. And laziness breeds insecurities and the need for validation. The kind of validation advertised in beer commercials and music videos.

People don't go to the zoo to see exotic animals; they go to the zoo to see how nature behaves when it doesn't have to pay rent at the end of the month. What do the animals do? They sit around doing nothing. The zebras, otters, elephants, tigers, and orangutans don't do a darn thing. Sure they have strong urges to mate and eat and occasionally fight over patriotic matters such as territory and females and spiritual matters such as really hot females, but other than that, animals just hang. They are alive just to exist, to be. At the core of our own humanity is this animal instinct to do nothing, to just sit around and be. The Zen-like state of zoo-animal existence, however, doesn't make anyone any money, which obnoxious men need if they ever wish to interact with females. So somewhere in the history of the human race, an idiot invented work, and thousands of years later millions upon millions of human beings are holed up in cubicles getting stressed out over things like sales trends and eating, drinking, smoking, and drugging themselves into big, fat, obese, unhealthy messes. It's ridiculous. It's sad. It's not natural.

All so the unsightly owners of your favorite professional sports teams can have beautiful wives with fake tits. Rioting basketball players and plastic surgery are, after all, what separates human beings from the animals. Another difference between humans and animals is that animals are not obese (unless they are pets of humans, which in turn opens them up to pyramid schemes and paternity lawsuits). Also, animals don't sit in a cubicle for fifty hours a week. Not only does the modern human lifestyle, or work style, encourage obesity, but it also encourages bad backs, carpal tunnel syndrome, decayed vision, bad posture, asthma, poor blood circulation, and that great American pastime: depression.

The good news is that despite the level of control corporate has over where you sit and for how long, there are some targeted exercises you can do to manage your weight, stress, stiffness, and general health while at your cubicle. So put on your favorite pink tank top beneath your work clothes and in your best Oprah Winfrey voice exclaim, "I love myself, so let's get started." Clap if you feel like it.

Disclaimer: We live in such a litigious society that plastic bags explain that they don't belong over your head, coffee cups quip in first-person narrative BE CAREFUL! I'M HOT!, and crosswalk lights flash luminescent numbers and beep at pedestrians because people can't figure out how not to get hit by oncoming traffic on a cloudless afternoon. So let it be known that, though the following techniques provide cubicle dwellers with commonplace workouts for combating stress and reducing the unhealthy consequences of a sedentary lifestyle, when you practice them you do so at your own risk. Many of these workouts are inspired by troubled acquaintances and questionable reaches of the Internet. There is no lifeguard on duty. Also, do not eat this book or try to use it as a towel. Otherwise, it's pretty harmless. Knock on wood.

Upper Body

When renowned French writer Victor Hugo published *The Hunchback of Notre Dame* in 1831, he had no idea how much his repugnantly postured, deaf bell ringer Quasimodo would have in common with legions of cubicle inhabitants in America. Despite incredible advances in technology and medicine, bad backs, sore necks, stiff shoulders, and lumbering gaits haunt the postures of millions of people who sit in cubicles and stare at computer screens. They lean forward.

CUBERS
INTERNATIONAL

Upper body

EMPLOYEE #: 34892378-012

They hunch. Like Quasimodo, they become part of the machinery. Below are some tips to help cubicle dwellers rediscover the upright, ambulatory beauty that evolution has bestowed upon our species. Perhaps one day cubicles will be as uncommon as bell towers.

OVERVIEW: It's hard to picture young Olympic gymnasts flying through the air and think grown adults would need advice on how to sit in a chair, but we do. Common sense be damned. Most pains and injuries in the cubicle community can be avoided by paying attention to your posture and ensuring bad habits are identified early and corrected. Your upper body should always be upright, with your head and neck in line with your spine. When typing or performing other office-related duties, bend forward from your hips, not your back. Slouching causes tension and strain, and reduces blood circulation.

RED-CARPET CHEST THRUST: Our culture demands that actresses have skinny bodies and big tits—and know how to flaunt both when walking down the red carpet before accepting the Maudlin Award for "best supporting actress in an ensemble of people addicted to painkillers." In addition to the cautionary tales actresses can teach us about raising our children, they can also teach us how to live healthier lives at our cubicles. The Red-Carpet Chest Thrust stretches your abdominal muscles, chest, and shoulders by mimicking that same shoulders-back, chest-forward posture actresses assume to promote their large breasts and toned shoulders when pacing down the red carpet as if they have a Jewish mother-in-law strapped to their backs. Yet there are a few other moves you can adapt to maximize the effectiveness of the exercise. Lock your fingers behind your head, then recline back in your chair; just be sure to do so without falling over or injuring yourself on a low or angular backrest. Now imagine the paparazzi pulverizing you with flashbulbs and shouts of "One more without the bra strap!" Keep your cool by breathing deeply, slowly inhaling and exhaling while moving your elbows toward each other and imagining butterflies scurrying across a prairie. Arch back so that your chest, back, and stomach muscles, if you have them, stretch. Your shoulder blades should close in together; if they actually touch, quit your job and join the circus. Hold that position and count to twenty-five while slowly exhaling away your anxiety. Calmly think of the people you are going to thank in your acceptance speech. Repeat the process as much as necessary, though never for more than two continuous hours. If you continue to feel discomfort and stress, consult the nearest physician for a painkiller prescription.

THE MINIATURE GOLF COURSE CHARACTER HEAD ROTATION: In a strange way, cubicle communities are every bit as surreal as miniature golf courses. The characters are more interesting than the game. All miniature golf courses, whether they are beachside or plunked in the middle of the cornfields of Iowa, have the creepy nine-foot clown, rusty hippopotamus, or polka-dotted dinosaur with a rotating head. The mechanized head slowly moves from one side to the other as a motor within its belly hums and bugs get fried in a zapper somewhere near a dropped ice cream cone. The job of a miniature golf course character can resemble that of a cubicle dweller: Its responsibilities are mundane and repetitive, and it works with some quirky and colorful colleagues. Furthermore, the same mechanized neck rotation maneuver is a great way for stressed and tense employees to relax. Every couple of hours or so, cubicle dwellers should close their eyes, clear their minds, and slowly turn their heads to the right for several seconds, then to the left. This action, when performed with Zen-like focus, reduces tension and blood pressure levels. Note: Don't swing your head around in a circle to reduce stress; it could screw up your vertebrae. And it looks weird.

DRUG-DEALER SIDEWALK NECK STRETCH: There comes a time in all drug dealers' careers when they have three police officers on top of them, pinning their heads against a cracked sidewalk with patches of crabgrass growing around its edges. Usually there is a chain-link fence nearby, and some empty beer cans. Occasionally an unkempt women in a bathrobe walks out of the woods to yell at the police. The Drug-Dealer Sidewalk Neck Stretch, however, is for loosening your neck muscles and relieving areas of stress. Slowly reach underneath your chair and lean forward, like you would if you thought your shoe were untied. Then place your right arm behind your back, as a police officer would if you were being arrested. Next, tilt your head to the left and a little forward, angling it so that you can look to the right to see if you effectively ditched your stash out of sight. Gently, as if convinced of your own innocence, inhale and exhale, while using your left hand to force your head toward your left shoulder. Count to twenty-five, or to fifteen in the foreign language you took in high school. Repeat, switching sides. If pain persists, plead insanity.

PERPLEXED SHOULDER CIRCLES: When tension builds in your upper body and shoulders, remain in a sitting position, stop everything, and drop your arms by your sides. Relax. Then, in a circular manner, rotate your shoulders. First slowly move them up and back about ten times, then slowly rotate them up and forward ten times. Keep your breathing constant and steady. If done properly, Perplexed Shoulder Circles will, at the top of the rotation, make you look as if a blind monk has just asked you, "How many light-years does it take a mouse running in a plastic ball to get to Jupiter?" Repeat these sets of ten two or three times. If you continue to feel stressed and anxious, try other tension-reducing exercises in this chapter, or get up and walk around outside for some fresh air. Don't stress yourself out by trying to answer that question . . . it's 45.989 light-years, considering the fact that mice in plastic balls rarely go in a straight line. According to Einstein's theory of relativity, by the time the mouse reaches Jupiter it will have died and been born again three times, reaching the planet's surface at the age of seven.

As with everything else in the cubicle community, remember that you are there to work and that personal health, no matter what the motivational posters or human resource people say, is secondary to the overall health of the corporate bottom line. So when you hear Richard Simmons in your heart and that creepy *Fitness Made Simple* John Basedow guy with the thin, muscular body and Photoshopped head in your mind, make sure that your cubicle workout doesn't garner unwanted attention. Take Todd Bukowkski, for example.

Three months ago Todd in the software development department asked Muriel Lipstank in cost-benefit analysis if she would go with him to a colleague's apartment party. Todd was turned down. He convinced himself that if he were only more buff, Muriel's answer would have been different. Todd knew he wasn't thinking like an idiot. He overheard Muriel talking to a co-worker in the kitchen about how hot Orlando Bloom is. "With a body like that," he heard her say, "I'd have his children tomorrow." Todd immediately joined an expensive gym, which he could afford by giving up breakfast and filling his car five dollars at a time. Also, he worked out at his cubicle. Women like Muriel, he knew, find dedication to one's health irresistibly sexy. Todd kept two unopened reams of legal-size paper on his desk to complement his calisthenics with curls, triceps exercises, and bench presses after adjusting his chair so he could lean back as if he were a working out in a recliner. To make his absolute dedication to health and exercise more conspicuous, Todd counted his repetitions aloud. He started every morning with Miniature Golf Course Character Head Rotations and Perplexed Shoulder Circles.

Todd's Adventures in Fitness
Cubicle 16-B, Thirty-third Floor. 9:30 AM.

Todd: One (Golf Course Character Head Rotation), shiiish! Two . . . shiiish. Three . . . shiiish. Push it! Push it! Four . . .

Aaron (Todd's cubicle neighbor): Dude, come on. You can turn your head side to side without making so much noise.

Todd: I'm . . . Five . . . shiiish . . . My body is a temple, man. Six . . . shiiish. No offense . . . Seven . . . shiiish, but don't be jealous just because I have discipline . . . Eight . . . Do it! Focus!

Aaron: What about the programming on the Artesque software package?

Todd: I'm finishing it up . . . Eight . . . shiiish . . . dammit, was that eight?

Aaron: I think you're on nine.

Todd: Nine . . . shiiish . . . well, we're a team, Aaron. Eight . . . shiiish. Why don't you start acting like it if you're just going to slouch around.

Aaron: Never mind. I'll do it.

Todd: Nine . . . shiiish . . . Cool.

9:45 AM.

Todd (on the phone): Hey, Muriel, I've got a question about the Artesque software package. It's important. You should come over so we can discuss it.

Muriel: So what's the issue, Todd?

Todd (leaning back in his chair, bench-pressing the reams of legal paper): Well . . . Seven . . . shiiish. Well, hold on . . . Eight . . . shiiish . . . I think there is a problem . . . Eight . . . shiiish . . . the HTML is so sloppy, it's like it was written by someone who couldn't program their way out of a wet paper bag.

Muriel: Well, Todd, that is your responsibility. Writing the code is your job.

Todd: My first responsibility is to my body. Eight . . . shiiish. I'm just here until I start my own business. Nine . . . shiiish. Shoot me your résumé if you're interested in a job. Nine . . . shiiish.

Muriel: I'll keep that in mind.

Todd (at Muriel's cubicle): Oh, hey, Muriel. Didn't realize I had walked this far during my cubicle workout cool-down. Got any tissues?

Muriel: Tissues?

Todd: Yeah, I've worked up a good sweat. Should probably check my pulse (places his fingers over his wrist). Pretty good.

Muriel: I'm sorry. But I don't have any tissues.

Todd (shaking his hands and rolling his neck): Yes, you do. They're in your left drawer.

Muriel: Oh, I forgot. Here.

Todd: Thanks (rips several tissues from the box and pats his forehead and neck). So anyway, maybe we should hang out sometime.

Muriel: No, thanks.

Todd: No, really. How about Saturday? I can pick you up at your apartment.

Muriel: Todd, I said no.

Todd (untucking his shirt from his pants and pulling it up to his chest): But look at my stomach. I've been working out. I'm almost as fit as Orlando Bloom. Here (stepping closer), feel my stomach!

Muriel: Gross! Todd, if you don't leave I'm filing an official complaint.

Todd: Fine! I hope you and your Hollywood boyfriend have fun together. You know, if he's an actor, you should write him a letter telling him you want to have his children. Hah! You live in such a fantasy world.

Muriel: Huh?

Todd: That's right. (Throws sweaty tissue into Muriel's trash can.)

Muriel: Eww.

Hands, Fingers, and Wrists

Spiritual and cerebral costs notwithstanding, the hands and wrists bear the brunt of cubicle life adversity. They perform, in the end, all of the typing, clicking, and scrolling that give life and meaning to our thoughts and inspirations. Countless hours in cubicles have brought a plague of bone, joint, and tendon ailments to thousands of cubicle inhabitants.

CUBERS INTERNATIONAL

Hands, fingers & wrists

EMPLOYEE #: 34892378-012

Though companies have made impressive efforts to provide ergonomic keyboards, chairs, and mice for America's hands and wrists, it is impossible to take away the repetitive and sedentary nature of the environment that wears down our fingers and what attaches them to our bodies.

OVERVIEW: Adjust your chair and desk so that your elbows rest on the armrests and your forearms extend onto, but not over, the keyboard. Ensure that your elbows are relaxed and your forearms are aligned with your wrists. Use every ergonomic option available, especially the mouse pad. You are not Ray Charles, so never bend your wrists up or down to type, or overextend them by reaching for double key functions. Here are some exercises to help keep your hands limber, healthy, and strong.

CUBE TIP

Use every ergonomic option available at your company, especially the mouse pad. Ergonomic mouse pads are cheap, are available everywhere, and provide excellent wrist support and preventive maintenance.

BOOGER FLICK: We all remember the toxic lumps of chewed gum and dispensed boogers that over the years accumulated like guano on the undersides of our high school desks. Well, for this exercise—which reduces tension and increases circulation in your arms and hands while also preventing carpal tunnel—you will need to recall awkward days of adolescence. At your cubicle, turn your hands so the palms face up, then press them on the underside of your desk. Now imagine it's your old high school desk decorated with fresh boogers strung along the underside like dollops of mint jelly. Remove your hands and, without allowing them to touch anything, shake the boogers off. Repeat the Booger Flick three times, especially if long hours of typing have caused your fingers, wrists, or forearms to ache.

DRUNK MONK: For this exercise, imagine you are a devout monk . . . after about nine beers. Sitting balanced and comfortably in your chair, bring your hands together with palms facing inward until they slightly press against each other, as if praying. Keep your elbows out and raised in the air. Then, like a drunk monk who can't control his hand coordination, let your right hand overpower your left hand, gently stretching it, again as if you are praying—but at an angle. Hold this position, calmly pretend to inhale and exhale incense, and count backward from forty-seven until you feel inner peace. Return your hands to their original position. Next, have your left hand overpower and stretch your right hand. Again, count until you feel inner peace. Ahhh.

SMELL MY PALMS: Though there is a good chance your knuckles may crack during this exercise, it may also stave off more disturbing forces such as carpal tunnel and stiffness. Loosely interlock your fingers and raise them, extending your elbows until your hands face outward in a *Hey, smell my palms* position. On calm, deliberate breaths, name the seven dwarfs in *Snow White*. Bring your hands to their original position and let them rest on your thighs, but not in a creepy manner. Repeat until your fingers, hands, and wrists feel as if they're connected with string cheese.

BEGGAR'S CLASP ROTATION: Though you don't have to get on your knees to perform this exercise, you do have to clasp your hands like a beggar asking for mercy, money, or simply three consecutive vacation days during the holiday season. Clench your hands together so the fingers are interlaced, and then whisper, "Please, God. I'll never drink again." Next, move your hands in a circular motion until the bones in your wrists and knuckles stop cracking. Then rotate them in the opposite direction until you are sure your joints and blood flow have been loosened up enough for another stint at the keyboard. But be careful when performing this exercise. You don't want to assume the begging position with a photo of Jessica Alba downloaded on your monitor.

Back

The expression *I got your back* is important to hear from friends, family, and colleagues, but in your cubicle this should be your chair's daily motto. In fact, good sturdy chairs are so essential that co-workers often steal them from one another, risking awkward confrontations and accusations about

their character. Even employees who refuse to steal binder clips from the stockroom find themselves furtively rolling a vacationing employee's chair down the hallway to their cubicle. Good office chairs are expensive, running easily into the several-hundred-dollar range. Stealing them is a crime, a serious one. Depending on which state you are in, chair theft can range from a Class 1 Misdemeanor to a Class 6 Felony. If you work for a Fortune 500 company, you are most likely committing a felony when stealing your colleague's (leather) chair. If you work for a government agency, chances are you're committing a misdemeanor when stealing your colleague's (folding) chair. Nevertheless, chair theft is a common crime because good chairs, especially those that are comfortably adjusted, are rare, and the demand is high. It's the perfect scenario for turning well-mannered and highly educated people into heartless, but good-postured, criminals.

OVERVIEW: Having a bad back is like falling down the stairs every time you breathe. Bad backs are detrimental not just because they are painful but because of the way they make people slow, if not ineffective, and grumpy at work. Even if you contort your body into an acceptable level of pain while seated in your cubicle, it's nearly impossible to maintain the same position for more than a few minutes. Bad backs lead to bad job situations. You can't fake your way through them. The best way to avoid a bad back is through proper posture, exercise, and, of course, chair selection.

THE CHAIR: Knowing when to pick your battles is an important skill to have when part of the cubicle community. And while others compete for bigger monitors, faster computer processors, or better parking spaces, save your employee negotiating capital for an adjustable chair that allows your feet to be flat on the floor with your knees bent at a healthy right (ninety-degree) angle. All companies want their employees to feel as if they are being treated equally and provide them with the same style, model, and make of office chair; yet, if you've established a reputation for being a noncomplainer and hard worker, management should consider your request. Sometimes you have to get your own back. Unlike kitchen chairs or the recliner in your den, office chairs should have an almost insect-like appearance: large, strong functional parts connected to one another by smaller strong parts. There should be a lower back (also known as lumbar) support that is sturdy and properly cushioned. There should be a broad, padded seat so you don't get biker or church-pew butt. Also, the chair should have five wheels that easily twist and roll with your movements so you can scuttle yourself into the hallway should you hear an inexplicable crashing sound. Office chairs with only three wheels provide less stability and mobility, and are generally less expensive. Also, the seat should have a smooth lazy-Susan spinning ability that allows for reaching, turning, or dizzying yourself into a drunken-type haze after mind-numbing staff meetings.

MIDLIFE CRISIS CRUNCHES: Nothing teaches us more about ourselves than the mistakes we make. And nothing can help us stretch our hips more than the posture we take upon learning that we have married the wrong person, chosen a miserable career, or wound up broke and loveless with three children failing out of school. For these calisthenics, adjust yourself in your chair so that you can lean forward without falling out. Next, place your right ankle on your left knee, as if you were watching a football game—both relaxed and concerned. Just as your team is about to score the winning field goal, your chilly wife reveals a pair of women's underwear she found in your car along with some lawyer's business card. "You have twenty-four hours to find yourself an apartment," she says. You put down your beer and place your right elbow on the inside of your right knee. Your double life is over. Breathe calmly and deeply. Push your right knee toward the ground so the outside portion of your right hip stretches. Hold this position while trying to name the last twenty Super Bowl champions. Then switch and perform the exercise on your left side. Figure out your next step in life. Cheer when your team scores the winning field goal. Finish your beer. Learn. Adjust. Make the best of the situation, just as you do with your life in a cubicle. Stretch. Don't stress.

WATERSKIING ACCIDENT ROTATION: Though this stretch may hurt when performed in a split second while waterskiing at forty-five miles an hour, at your cubicle desk it can do wonders for your lower back, glutes, and hips. For this exercise, place your right ankle on your left knee as if you were performing Midlife Crisis Crunches. Instead of placing your right elbow on the inside of your knee, however, wrap your left arm around your right knee, as if you were going to give it a noogie. While keeping your back straight, as if you were waterskiing, perform a controlled "fall" by pulling your knee toward your chest while turning your body to the right. Swivel as far to the right as possible, breathing steadily. You should feel the muscles in your back, legs, and hip stretch; use your right arm to extend the strain, but don't overdo it. Repeat the process on your left side. Go slowly and smoothly. Remember, just because it's an accident in slow motion doesn't mean you can't hurt yourself.

Stomach and Abdomen

There is no greater testimony to the failure of the American educational system than the fact that our citizens watch infomercials promoting oversize rubber bands and padded bicycle handlebars as exercise equipment—and happily give the sellers $29.95 over the next three months for the stuff. Yes, our consumer-driven society encourages us to supersize our waistlines, and then that same society turns against us like some jealous mother-in-law who, with a rolled-up copy of *People* magazine in her hands, berates us for being fat, ugly, and worthless. Full of guilt and shame, we give our savings to anyone on television with an idea, pill, or contraption that can make us fit again. What the companies are doing, of course, is turning us against ourselves. They want us to be fat. They want us to be skinny. There is good money in both. What they don't want is for us to be happy.

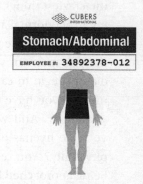

Fortunately, this is America, and you get to decide whether or not you are happy. If having a flabby gut makes you unhappy, then there are some steps you can take, even if you work in a cubicle. Remember, as with other exercises and breakfast cereal, these techniques alone will not result in significant changes. They must be part of a balanced, healthy lifestyle.

OVERVIEW: For many cubicle workers, the stomach is divided into four parts: the gut, two love handles, and back fat. For buff cubicle inhabitants, the stomach is divided into three parts: the six-pack abdominal muscles, the condescending attitude, and that unfortunate barbed-wire tattoo on the upper arm, which is an extension of the abdominal muscles. "Dude, this tattoo is so cool. No one anywhere has one like it." (Ahh, 1998 was the cruelest of years.) Nevertheless, there is hope for those in the first category who desire to trim down their stomachs without having to get a tattoo or hate third-world countries for being so lazy and not using condoms.

THE HOTTIE HELLO: Most of us understand that the opposite sex can make us do crazy things like throw bread sticks in an Italian restaurant, fill out a police report over a missing T-shirt, or crash our car into a second-story bedroom. Some of the craziest things we do, however, occur when we're attempting to act normal around the opposite sex. For example, you've just met someone you're particularly attracted to. Naturally, in the one moment you have to impress that person, you immediately begin to catalog every insecurity in your psyche, every mistake you have made in your life, and every ounce of fat on your body. And while emotionally your fears are feeding on you like hyenas on a zebra carcass, what's happening to you physically? You're assuming the same posture as if you were being approached by a stegosaurus. Even if you don't have any you flex your ab muscles, tightening them as much as possible. This, of course, will force you to hold your breath. Then, with the last pockets of air left in your lungs, you exhale and say something like, "I have two credit cards." Inhale. Go to the stairwell and yell at yourself for being such an idiot. Compose yourself. Return to your cubicle. Sit in your chair and do the exact same thing to your stomach muscles about ten times, rest for thirty seconds, and then repeat. You do not, clearly, have to say anything or try to impress yourself or get a date with yourself, even though those will be your plans this weekend.

THE CULINARY LUDDITE: Everyone has been preached to about the importance of being active and not succumbing to the indolent, sedentary life endemic to cubicle work. Well, sometimes the best thing you can do for your stomach and overall health is to remain seated at your cubicle. Sure, the fine makers of candy bars, soft drinks, and that exotic Chinese export, Cup Noodles, want you to relax on the couch of their comfort food, but resist the temptation. Vending machines with all their marketing and technology are the enemy. Keep healthy snacks at your desk—granola bars, carrot sticks, and other natural products. Don't fall for the flashy "Now with Calcium" marketing crud. And especially don't be sucked in by vending machines with life-affirming bright colors in the drably decorated office kitchen. Don't put any money in that glowing high-tech vending machine with the appealing images of iced drinks and illuminated chemical-filled candies, or that multi-shelved contraption that dispenses easy unhealthy fixes for temporary cravings. If your office kitchen offers the same food as a truck-stop gas station, ask human resources how many miles to Bangor, Maine. Explain that creepy hedge-fund managers in Manhattan have their own chefs who cook healthy, personal meals that include steamed asparagus and shiitake mushrooms. Surely trying to make an honest, virtuous living deserves honest, virtuous meals and snack options. Why must you take the time to push B-17 and get nothing but a chilled cheeseburger trapped in the corner of a glorified refrigerator? Tell them you are a Culinary Luddite and despise the fact that technology can send a live lobster from Maine to Shanghai, but you can't get a fresh turkey-and-lettuce sandwich. Do they care or not? Demand better options. Reduce the size of your stomach by exercising your brain and your self-esteem.

Legs

Sci-fi movies often feature superclairvoyant heroes who don't have limbs, torsos, or even necks. This is every corporation's vision of a perfect future—employees who are nothing more than human heads in amniotic-fluid-filled glass jars

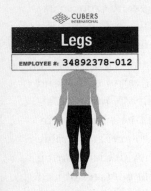

that can process quarterly reports and create management profiles with utmost efficiency. Like other parts of your body and psychology, it is up to you, not the company, to care for them. If you don't, you'll only have yourself to blame when you receive holiday cards of your grandchildren and they're nothing more than heads in jars stacked on top of one another next to a snowman.

OVERVIEW: Legs are a very sexy part of the human body, and they do garner attention whether you are a man or woman. Wear something classy to cover, or partially cover, your lower half. It's okay to be sexy, but not slutty. Don't pretend your legs are a pet poodle that you can't control from prancing around barking at people. No one likes those who imply they don't want attention and then dress as if they belong in a glass box in Amsterdam. Men should save the tight pants for the return of

1977, and women should reserve miniskirts for when old age and dementia has them believing they are eighteen again. Also, if you work out during lunch, don't walk back into the office in your sweaty shorts or spandex pants. Everyone feels sexier after a good workout, but that doesn't mean strutting around the cubicle community in your revealing exercise clothes is sexy. It's actually pretty distracting . . . in a bad way.

THE DELIVERANCE STRETCH: No one at work likes to be told to bend over, but that is exactly what you need to do to keep your legs healthy as a cubicle dweller. Cubicle existence is about sitting down, so atrophy is the primary concern regarding the health of your legs. When you have free time and feel no one is watching you, simply stand up from your chair and touch (or try to touch) your toes. Bend over at your waist and stretch slowly and smoothly so that you feel the pull in your calves and hamstrings—just like your eighth-grade gym teacher taught you. Don't bounce, rush, or force your stretch. Vary the exercise by spreading your feet; stretch your inner thighs by slowly rotating your torso while attempting to touch your toes. Next, lean back and stretch your quadriceps; do this when colleagues are not around, or run the risk of hearing comments such as, "Now squeal like a pig." Also, don't think you're at home or in the gym and use your desk or chair as equipment to assist your stretching exercises. There is a good reason your cubicle does not look like a Bowflex machine.

THE POLITICIAN: Great political leaders know how to turn every waking moment into an opportunity to promote themselves. When you feel your legs becoming cramped or tingly, or simply forget they're there, take them for a spin. While you're at it, seize the opportunity to check in with colleagues and spend face-to-face time with them. Shake their hands. Ask how they are doing. Ask if there is anything you can do for them. Learn about their needs, their backgrounds, and what their families are like. Eventually they will look forward to your forays around the cubicle community. You will create a reputation for being proactive, responsible, and caring. Just don't tell them that you're really exercising. Voters don't want the truth. Voters want to feel good.

Eyes

Without our eyes we wouldn't be able to see, and without being able to see there would be no way for corporations, politicians, and media outlets to convince us that what we're actually seeing isn't real. They want us to believe in their make-believe world, to see through their prescription lenses. In

reality, the chiseled men who drink Coke and Pepsi in television commercials don't look like the men you work with who drink Coke and Pepsi. That politician who claims to come from a blue-collar upbringing just ordered red wine at a diner. According to the news only pedophiles and blond murder victims constitute important breaking stories. Everyone wants to see things for you. Take a look around for yourself.

OVERVIEW: Sometimes, when employees become overworked and stressed, their eyes turn bloodshot and are enveloped by dark circles. These symptoms are the first signals that employees are becoming cubicle zombies—a process in which educated and talented professionals are turned into lifeless bodies void of personality, humor, perspective, and creativity. Sadly, most cubicle dwellers remain unaware of a few simple eye exercises they can do to prevent themselves from becoming the living dead.

SIMPLE EYE EXERCISES: Cubicle dwellers can do wonders for their eye health just by closing them for several seconds. Do this intermittently, and your eyes will thank you by not hallucinating that your e-mails are written in Sanskrit or that you're holding three coffee cups in your hand. Just like you, your eyes need to get away every now and then. So let them wander. Look at things in the distance. Spin around in your chair and take in your surroundings for a few seconds. And most important, have your monitor properly positioned. Do not place your monitor so that you have to look up at it, peer down on it, or tilt your head—and eyes—in any way. Make sure nothing obstructs your view of the monitor, such as computer speakers, fast-food bags, or mugs filled with pens and pencils. The top edge of the monitor should be at eye level and within reach so that it doesn't strain your eyes to look at it or strain your arms to adjust it. Also, if reflected light from overhead fixtures or unfiltered windows bothers your eyes, ask your administrative support for a glare guard.

PYGMALION GLANCES: Checking on the health of your eyes is not a narcissistic exercise; it is a prudent one. So affix a small mirror (see chapter 8) to your monitor and look in it occasionally to gauge the level of tiredness in and around your eyes. Your eyes will let you know when they are tired. They will ache. They will have difficulty focusing. They will retreat into your head like a couple of rats and leave dark circles and wrinkles where your youth used to shine. Unfortunately, cubicle employees often ignore or simply do not recognize when their eyes are in distress. Getting into the habit of checking on their condition several times during the workday will help in assessing their health. Your eyes will tell you what you are seeing.

Break Time

Nearly every exercise mentioned in this chapter can be replaced by one simple action: taking a break. Some employees don't like to take breaks because they believe it appears to others as if they are avoiding work. These employees are doing themselves a disservice and will, ironically, pay the price for such dedication in the long run by having to take sick days in order to repair their exhausted bodies and souls. Every thirty minutes or so, cubicle inhabitants should do some form of seated exercise or simply stand up and walk around. Visit a friend. Mingle in the kitchen. Go to the bathroom even if you don't have to. Sneak off to the stairwell and do some jumping jacks. If possible, schedule time to hit the gym during the workday—at lunch, for example. If the gym is too crowded at noon, try to negotiate another lunch hour. Getting up and walking around is like taking your eyes out for some fresh air, and is an invigorating change from being forced to look at glowing monitor screens for unnatural lengths of time. In general, movement is great for your legs, back, torso, posture, upper body, neck, and brain. While you're up, take a few seconds to stretch your arms and hands; bend down and touch your toes. Also, walking around and visiting colleagues can help your career as long as your visits are friendly, professional, and welcome. Being social can be a great professional move and improve psychological health by creating friendships, increasing job security through networking, and generally amping up self-esteem and a sense of belonging.

Have a Life

As the saying goes, *Don't mistake having a career for having a life.* The healthiest exercise a cubicle inhabitant can perform is to become a well-rounded person. Love yourself and others. Take risks. Call your family, even if you hate them. Remember your friends' birthdays. E-mail that person from high school you've lost touch with. Tell people about your life. Confide in others. If they burn you, they burn you. Rise from the ashes. On the day you die, many from work will miss your presence and your work personality, but the trick to life is having people miss you for your soul, your true being. The unfortunate reality about work is that even though you spend much of your life there, you are not yourself there. It's sad but true. You have to edit your feelings and your language. Sometimes being a professional means being able to hide your true thoughts, feelings, and opinions. That sort of oppression, of course, will make anyone tired, depressed, and frustrated.

The only way to keep your sanity in this type of situation is to have a life outside of the corporate confines, and don't let corporations into it. The very soul of America depends on our personal lives being personal. Companies will try to convince you that what is best for them is best for you. Resist their version of the world and their version of your life. Don't confuse being a professional person with being a good person. Know who your real family is.

Quick Quiz Self-Assessment

(1) Last Tuesday Kevin Warren, an affiliate relations officer, forgot to empty the dishwasher, something his wife said he

should do "just to acknowledge her existence." Also, she explained, while in the kitchen he should "say hello to the maid wearing his wedding ring." Kevin did neither; happy hour intervened. So he has spent the ensuing nights sleeping on the pullout couch, which has given him a sore neck and sleep deprivation. Which of the following cubicle exercises should he do to alleviate his pain?

    (a) Red-Carpet Chest Thrust

    (b) Midlife Crisis Crunches

    (c) Booger Flick

    (d) Perplexed Shoulder Circles

    (e) Pygmalion Glances

    (f) Drug-Dealer Sidewalk Neck Stretch

    (g) Drunk Monk

    (h) The Hottie Hello

    (i) Deliverance Stretch

(2) Which of the following are *not* desirable features in an office chair?

    (a) Solid, wooden seat with carved-out indentations for butt cheeks.

    (b) Constructed of separate and adjustable pieces for flexibility and maneuverability.

    (c) Single-piece construction to avoid loose pieces and weak joints.

    (d) Padded lower-back and seat sections.

    (e) Five wheels for stability and mobility.

    (f) Tall enough so your feet dangle, preventing leg cramping.

(3) Darren Adibi went to an all-male grade school, an all-male high school, and a small, all-male liberal arts college in New England. Though he has had two serious girlfriends in his life, he has never seen a young woman like Karen Frost.

She is sexy, intelligent, and can talk football like a sports anchor. Everyone at Cubers International wants to nail her. Last Monday morning Darren was alone on the elevator when Karen suddenly stepped in just before the doors closed. "Hello, Darren," she said, turning toward him. "How was your weekend?" Which cubicle exercise below most resembles Darren's immediate reaction?

(a) The Politician

(b) The Miniature Golf Course Head Rotation

(c) Smell My Palms

(d) The Hottie Hello

(e) Waterskiing Accident Rotation

(f) Beggar's Clasp Rotation

ANSWERS:
(1) f. Drug-Dealer Sidewalk Neck Stretch. (2) a, c, f. (3) d. The Hottie Hello.

CHAPTER TEN

Protecting Yourself and Your Cubicle

Protection Begins with Awareness

Without using unappealing corporate reality as an excuse to have a bad attitude, or blaming capitalism for your and society's problems, understand that you are responsible for your professional and personal happiness. Educate yourself. Know your cubicle surroundings and learn the nature of the business environment. Never complain. Even good jobs go bad. Great bosses quit. Close friends get fired. Boutique businesses merge with gargantuan, impersonal conglomerates. All you have control over is you and your attitude—how you deal with reality. So sit up straight and smile: No one gives a crap about you, especially not people with designer watches and company-funded subscriptions to *The Wall Street Journal*.

Don't be misled by your plastic-coated employee ID, your parking pass, or the access card that beeps you through self-locking doorways. It's nothing personal. Corporate security is designed to protect the interests of the company, and protecting the interests of the company often means, subsequently, protecting the company's employees. Just because the company sees you as an asset doesn't mean the company sees you as a person. Be thankful for the protection corporate provides. Be positive. But don't be a fool. Don't be lulled into a false sense of security. Learn to look out for yourself and protect your belongings, identity, and privacy from those you work for and with. Just remember to smile while doing so.

Protecting Your Stuff

You lock your car doors and store valuables in the trunk just in case. The windows of your house are wired into a home security system with a direct connection to the police. The lights on your porch have motion sensors. You've installed an extra bolt lock on the side garage door just in case someone loves your tool collection as much as you do. Yet at work you leave your wallet on your desk while visiting the bathroom. You hang your purse from a cubicle hook where you can't even see it. You promised your IT people that you would take good care of the company laptop, and when you returned from the quick meeting down the hall, it was gone. Try not to be paranoid, but be smart. Though cubicle communities may feel safe and antiseptic, they are still filled with people, and people, well, they're filled with emotions and impulses. Disgruntled employees feel the need to get even, and may do so by stealing from their colleagues. Every holiday season your local news will run a story about a thief who entered through a parking garage door and made off with cell phones and laptops. Sometimes the temptation of easy money gets the better of people whom we've always considered honorable. Other times people don't take their medication and act out of character. For whatever reason, don't think that human nature stops at the company elevator.

The interview process, despite its best efforts, does not always see people's dark sides or their proneness to folly and idiocy. Whenever something goes missing, stay cool. Don't overreact. Don't be an idiot. Don't be a racist or a snob. Don't suggest it was the cleaning staff because you think they are poor and desperate. Don't accuse Dan Bolger in business valuation because you heard he had a drug problem and probably needs money if he is relapsing. Don't blame the building security people or system for not watching out for your things. Blame, but don't kill, yourself. These things happen, especially when you're not prepared or paying attention. So take the necessary steps to protect your stuff and your sanity. If you're the type that hates sitting with a wallet in your back pocket, store it somewhere safe, like a lockable desk drawer. Do the same with ID cards and access passes if you don't keep them on your person. Don't stow your purse somewhere you can't see it. Just because it's in your cubicle and near you doesn't mean it's beyond the reach of unscrupulous people. Keep it in sight. Same goes for laptops and cell phones. Always keep your belongings, from your car keys to your umbrella, somewhere safe. Get into a routine of placing your valuables in the same secure location every morning. Protect yourself by securing your routine.

Protecting Your Identity

You guard your identity. But you write your password on a Post-it note and stick it to your monitor. While discussing your phone bill with customer service you repeat your birth date and Social Security number within earshot of a dozen people. Your trash can holds all your credit card information. You jeopardize your reputation and job security every day by nonchalantly visiting questionable Internet sites without knowing who may be watching you. Remember that the Internet is public territory. If there is a naked woman on your monitor screen, she is not some pornographic stranger that visited your computer; she is your companion, your naked date in stilettos, that you idiotically brought to work thinking only you could see her. Well, others can see her, lots of others. And your date doesn't mind. She's not embarrassed. She's not in trouble. Unlike you, she's just doing her job.

PASSWORDS ARE SECRETS: Sure, we all forget our passwords at one time or another for one reason or another. Having to remember your boyfriend's holiday party, your daughter's soccer league schedule, your father-in-law's birthday, and your nephew's school play, it's no wonder you have trouble remembering your passwords. Don't worry; you're not going senile or insane. Passwords are, unfortunately, a necessary inconvenience in modern life, one needed to protect us from unprincipled people. To make matters even worse, like the keys on your key chain, we have multiple passwords that allow us entry into areas of our own personal lives. You have a work password to log on to your computer. You have a personal password to view your personal e-mails. You have passwords that give you access to online banking so you can manage your various accounts, pay your cable, phone, and utility bills, buy and sell stocks, trade fantasy baseball players when they get injured, and purchase anything from groceries to SUVs. Over time many of us get lackadaisical and feel as if nothing bad is ever going to happen to us. Crime, after all, is something that happens to other people. You live in a safe neighborhood. You work for a nice company. So you begin to take shortcuts. You hide a house key under the welcome mat or under the potted geranium on the front steps. No one would ever look there. You write your password on an old lunch receipt and store it behind the box of paper clips in your desk drawer. No one would ever check there, either. Thankfully you use the same password for all of your online business and personal activities. So even if the "Remember Password" function is erased because an IT intern deleted all your cookies last night while installing new software, you are covered. Then a bill from a credit card you never applied for, but has your name, shows up in your mail. Apparently, last month, while you were in the final negotiations for the Rayburn deal, you bought four cases of Milwaukee's Best, twelve rolls of fun-print Bounty paper towels, three packs of Marlboro Reds, and a Hershey's Mr. Goodbar. You're lucky that this "you" couldn't carry anything more, or didn't have a taste for fine caviar and pinot grigio. Congratulations. Many of us complain that there aren't enough hours in the day to get done what needs to be done; that if only we had a clone, we could be everything to everyone. Well, be careful what you ask for. In the dark world of identity theft, your twin is less like *Full House* and more like *Full Metal Jacket*. If you use the same password for all your accounts, you've provided the criminal with every key to every door in your house of cyber activity. Cyber thieves in the wire.

Create a system for your passwords so that they are all different, thus limiting the amount of damage that can be done should your information fall into the wrong hands. Do not follow a simple pattern to create your passwords. For example, if you are an accountant, and hackers break into a site you frequent and steal your personal information—including your password, which happens to be "accountant1"—then they are smart enough to assume that you were lazy enough to make your next password "accountant2"; then "accountant3"; and so on. Furthermore, employees often make the mistake of creating their passwords from personal information such as their own names, their spouse's names, their birthdays, or their children's names. And for the love of humanity, do not use "password" as your password. Don't be predictable when so much is at stake. If you think memorizing or safely storing your password information is difficult, try reclaiming your identity. Try visiting the Department of Motor Vehicles to renew your license, only to find out that you don't exist. Try convincing creditors, vendors, and lenders that you are not you, that you are somebody else pretending to be you. So devise a password system that is relatively complex, cryptic, and uniquely sensible to you. Use various letters and numbers. Store them in separate, safe locations. And no, your wallet and purse are not separate, safe locations. Neither is your monitor or your desk drawer. Page 124 of your personal Major League Baseball directory in your cubicle cabinet is a decent place. Be creative with how you create and choose to hide your passwords. It may be the difference between you or someone else with your name vacationing in the Pocono Mountains this spring. An essential part of being a professional cubicle inhabitant is knowing how to handle confidential information responsibly, especially passwords. Don't be the employee who has to slink into the IT department and explain that your password was stolen, along with your identity, and your reputation.

BROADCASTING: As mentioned in previous chapters, it is unwise to discuss personal issues within earshot of colleagues. Revealing personal details about your friendly or intimate relationships, financial or emotional hardships, or lack of respect for your work could harm—if not ruin—your professional standing. It is equally foolish to openly discuss confidential details that are connected to your finances. Sure, chances are the people you work with share your moral and ethical values. But don't forget that cubicle communities are also transient settings where contractors, cleaning and maintenance staff, collaborators from other companies, friends and family of colleagues, and downright strangers often pass through. So be careful when you are on the phone or shopping online. If you must tell someone your credit card number and expiration date, your Social Security number, or any sort of password over the phone, be sure to speak softly and preferably when no one, or as few people as possible, are around. When ordering online, be sure that no one is watching you. Be sure that you are prepared and efficient so you don't have to leave your credit card lying around or your personal information on your monitor while trying to complete the transaction. Also, when you print out a confirmation of your purchase, make sure the receipt isn't left in the printer tray for your colleagues to accidentally pick up and pass around the office.

Don't-Mess-with-My-Stuff Tactics

Most neighborhood break-ins occur while residents are out of town, gone fishing, or spending some of their hard-earned money enjoying dinner and a movie. Neighborhood thieves like to take things when no one is around. Cubicle thieves are no different. They, too, like to abscond with property when you are not there to guard it. Sure, your grandmother's silver brooch and your high school ring may hold more sentimental and monetary value than your favorite pair of scissors or worn-in office chair, but the feeling of being violated is never a positive one. Perhaps even more disconcerting is that when your home is broken into, it is easy to imagine some stranger with a flashlight tossing your wife's underwear around the bedroom in search of jewelry. A cubicle crime, however, is most likely perpetrated by someone you know well who casually swept past your cubicle and made a fast, easy, well-planned strike. In a mythological cubicle community, these things never happen. In a well-managed cubicle community, cubicle inhabitants have a sense of humor about these things happening. In a poorly managed cubicle community, these thefts become a black-market currency of illegally obtained and traded merchandise. In fact, some employees have been known to make a nice side living by profiting from the black-market office supplies trade, often dealing in dark alleyways where underground godfathers of stolen office supplies organize raids, hits, and money-laundering opportunities before adjourning to small Italian restaurants. It is up to you individually to protect your belongings and to prevent them from being stolen, traded, and resold to illegal Chinese merchants. Here are some suggestions for keeping your cubicle belongings where they belong.

LOCKDOWN: The term *lockdown* is a colloquialism taken from jail lingo meaning "event in which deputies wrestle inmates to the floor and body-search them with the same rubber gloves later used by the inmates to cut tomatoes and have kitchen intercourse." During lockdown all general-population inmates must report to their cells, all doors are electronically locked, and every loose item—be it book, basketball, or pencil—must be dropped or placed in its rightful location immediately. In essence, it's a time to intimidate inmates and remind them that at any moment they can be subdued, humiliated, and reminded of who, and where, they are.

Leaving for vacation, cubicle employees can put their own belongings in a similar state of "lockdown." By making your workstation brutally organized, inaccessible, and impenetrable, you discourage others from entering your cubicle before the impulse for criminal behavior has time to form in their heads. For example, vacationing employees can leave a police baton, or perhaps a police flashlight and pair of rubber gloves, beside their keyboard. If you have them, handcuffs are a nice touch, even the fake-silver plastic ones; they look real. These props convincingly convey the idea of "lockdown" and will surely deter potential thieves from traversing across the cubicle's missing fourth wall. In fact, they may never come back to your cubicle again.

THREE MILE CUBICLE: Creating the image that your cubicle area is diseased, infected, and somehow unhealthy will prevent even the most sinister co-worker from breaking into your cubicle and personal things. As learned in the Three Mile Island section of chapter 7, creating the appearance of potential harm can be enough to keep unwanted elements away. Of course, when you're on vacation you can't be there to personify the calamity: yet, you can set up a few props in your cubicle that will effectively create a disaster scenario. Fashioning your cubicle disaster after an industrial disaster, rather than a natural disaster, is preferable because it's a better aesthetic match with the insensitive corporate environment. But be sensible; the most frightful chemicals and diseases are those we can't see or smell. Unleashing a prop such as Bengay while you are away for a week would incite a mob thrashing of your cubicle. Instead place an open tube of cortisone, some crumpled paper towels, and perhaps a couple of slices of moldy wheat bread on a paper plate near your keyboard. Hemorrhoid creme is always good, too. And make sure to leave the cap off with perhaps a smudge on an open tissue for added effect. Neosporin is also effective— and so versatile that it leads to speculation. Vaseline is deliciously enigmatic. A few unopened tubes of Compound W are also a nice touch, like baby's breath in a flower bouquet. Use your imagination. When you're gone, the criminals will use theirs. Bank on it.

YELLOW POLICE TAPE: Unfortunately, the human race is violent and prone to crime. Cubicle communities, however, are some of the safest environments on the planet. Crafty cubicle dwellers know to use the image of violence and crime to their advantage, particularly when they are not around to guard their property. The specter of crime can be an effective deter-

rent where people live in a bubble of safety. American pop culture is fixated on murders, forensic science, and courtroom dramas in which Hollywood actors play regular people who actually have to pay for their crimes.

Employees across America begin their mornings discussing last night's *Law and Order* episode about a double murder where a set of fraternal twins were found covered in pancake mix, wrapped up in a *Shrek*-themed sleeping bag, and doused in maple syrup. The murderer turned out to be an employee at KFC who was driven insane by a low-carb diet. The KFC, and the 8-square-mile scene of the crime were all cordoned off with yellow police tape that read CRIME SCENE INVESTIGATION DO NOT CROSS. The community, of course, was outraged by the irresponsible use of yellow police tape. Business owners claimed

!

Don't be afraid to look a little paranoid when it comes to protecting your property. Though some co-workers may poke fun at the fact that you always lock your cubicle cabinets and desk drawers, when the unexpected crook passes through, you will look like the smartest person in your cube community. Most, if not all, of your colleagues probably have no idea where the key(s) to their cabinets and drawers are—if they're even aware they can be locked. Make locking your valuables in a sturdy cabinet or drawer a habit every morning. You'll sleep better at night. Just remember to keep your key in a safe place, like your pocket, throughout the workday.

the yellow police tape was driving away customers. Though none of the actors in the show comes across as even remotely human, the point about yellow police tape is accurate.

Lots of research goes into these crime-solver programs. People hate the yellow police tape. It scares them. It drives down property values. It makes people wonder what crime happened, whom it happened to, and if they are next. This is why yellow police tape is so effective in the cubicle community. On the day before your vacation, make sure all of your responsibilities are covered, then log off your computer, take out some stolen yellow police tape, and tack as many strips as possible across the cubicle entrance. The colleagues who know you are on vacation will get the point; those who don't know you are on vacation will become interested in you. Even the ones who always avoided making eye contact with you in the hallway. They will ask about you. "What happened to Janet over in marketing? Is she okay?" Others will theorize. "I heard she ran a cockfighting ring in her cubicle after hours. She walled off the entrance in chicken wire, dropped in some roosters, and broadcast the fight over the Web from that video camera on top of her monitor. Rumor has it Bob and Nathan are being investigated as well. Ever notice how neither of them ever knows about any television shows? They don't even know who Sam Waterston is. You know they're up to no good at night."

"No way, maybe they'll make a show about it. Do you think we can be extras in it?"

"Maybe. All I know is to stay away from her cubicle. Nothing but bad news in there."

"Don't worry. I was eyeing her chair, but I'm not going near her cube."

BODY OUTLINE: Again, thanks to television, movies, and America's obsession with murder, everyone knows three things about murder scenes: (1) Most people know their murderers, (2) stealing semen from the sperm bank and leaving it at the crime scene will make anyone a free man, and (3) the police always outline in chalk where the dead body was found. The Body Outline cubicle protection technique is easy. Before logging off and leaving for vacation, take some masking tape from the supply closet and make an outline of a dead body in your cubicle. Be creative. Don't use the hackneyed adult-size fetal position or the crucifix position on the floor. Though it may take more time, make it more authentic by outlining a dead body half on your desk and half on the floor. Turn it upside down, or perhaps feature a missing leg, then create a masking-tape outline of a leg somewhere in the kitchen or down the hallway. Have fun with your murder victim. Don't go as far as laying down fake bloodstains with ketchup, but do provide other convincing props: a hammer, crumpled-up Chinese hand fan, bent golf club, broken water ski, glove that doesn't fit your hand, or—that ever-popular network news shot—the random shoe.

Make sure the laces are untied. Unfortunately, police and FBI training programs only require that their students read textbooks on forensic science and fingerprinting. If they had studied Cinderella and matching crime scene shoes with feet, many of our heinous predators would be behind bars. Whether or not you decide to go with the shoe option, the Body Outline cubicle protection technique is easy and effective, particularly for those sudden, unexpected occasions that require time off from work.

MOOD MANIPULATION: Don't advertise your upcoming vacation. Tame happy emotions about approaching leave time. Colleagues who know when your leave is scheduled will plan as soon as they can how to steal from you what they want. These plans are often very elaborate. Chairs being the Holy Grail of office theft, cunning co-workers know to plan "malfunctions" of their own chairs ahead of time. The best schemers have their chairs break during busy moments, when everyone around understands that there is an elevated stress level and that replacing a dysfunctional chair is not only acceptable but necessary. So avoid informing your colleagues of your week at Sandals in the Bahamas or your skiing trip to Steamboat. Even the most goodhearted employees get jealous at 2 PM on Wednesday when they have to cover for you and imagine you lounging on the beach or slinging down a ski slope. It's human nature. So you'd better plan for it. When people get jealous, it makes it easier for them to rationalize criminal behavior. The trick in life is to minimize the circumstances where employees can find themselves in this frame of mind. So don't brag about your great vacation. Don't advertise how great it will be to get away from the office and relax or do something adventurous. Be just as miserable on the day before your vacation as on the day you get back.

Bad Example of Hiding an Upcoming Vacation
Cubicle 19-Q, Second Floor. 11:01 AM.

Myra Beckson (who took two years of French and Spanish in high school, and is leaving for Barcelona tomorrow morning): Hey, Ted. Thanks for coming over. I've been looking at this Covington Fund audit and think we should change some of the formatting.

Ted Holmes: But we don't file that audit until the twenty-fifth. That's almost two weeks away.

Myra Beckson: I know, but I'm going to Español tomorrow and want to finish all this up before I leave. Who knows, in the sexiest city in the world I just might not come back! Ah, Sangria City! Here I come!

Ted Holmes: Oh, well, that's great, Myra. Have fun. That's good that you're getting everything tied up before you go.

Myra Beckson: Well, there is still tons of number crunching to be done on the Woolspin project. But mentally, I'm not even here. I've already checked out.

Ted Holmes: That's good to know. Where did you get that hanging file rack?

Myra Beckson: From office supplies. They only had about three of them and I was lucky enough to get one. All you have to do is complain enough. Squeaky wheel gets the oil.

Ted Holmes: I'll keep that in mind. So am I the one getting the Woolspin project when you're gone?

Myra Beckson: Doubtful. Dale said it will probably be farmed out to Maureen or Seth. They won't care about all the extra work. They'll probably think it's a compliment. Like the company trusts them with more responsibility. I love new employees. They're so gullible.

Ted Holmes: Maureen and Seth have been here longer than I have.

Myra Beckson: *Disculpe moi la bouche, amigo.*

Ted Holmes: Huh?

Myra Beckson: That's Spanish—actually, Catalonian—for "I knew that, mister."

Ted Holmes: Oh, anyway. Have a great trip.

Myra Beckson: *Au jus, mí amor.*

Ted Holmes (in his head): *Thanks for the hanging file rack.*

Great Example of Hiding an Upcoming Vacation
Cubicle 19-Q, Second Floor. 11:01 AM.

Myra Beckson (who took two years of French and Spanish in high school, and is leaving for Barcelona tomorrow morning): Hey, Ted. Thanks for coming over. I've been looking at this Covington Fund audit and think we should change some of the formatting.

Ted Holmes: But we don't file that audit until the twenty-fifth. That's almost two weeks away.

Myra Beckson: I know, but my schedule gets hectic and I won't be available over the next several weeks. So I just want to stay on top of things.

Ted Holmes: Sounds like you have everything under control. Let me know if you need any help.

Myra Beckson: Well, there's still tons of number crunching to be done on the Woolspin project. I may need to do a little delegating on that account. I'll have to check with Dale first.

Ted Holmes: Okay, just let me know. Where did you get that hanging file rack?

Myra Beckson: From office supplies. I've been having trouble organizing all of these accounts and thought a hanging file rack would help. It's great. I can keep each account separate and locate each one at a glance. No more sorting through unruly stacks. You should put in a request for one if you think it would help. I might have an extra request form around here if you need one.

Ted Holmes: Thanks, I'll keep that in mind. I might just do that if things get out of control. Since your schedule is full, do you think I'll get the Woolspin project?

Myra Beckson: Doubtful. Dale said he'll probably bring in Maureen or Seth to help out. They're still a little green and could benefit from some more hands-on experience with these accounts.

Ted Holmes: Maureen and Seth have been here longer than I have.

Myra Beckson: Oh, I'm sorry, Ted. Really? Well, please take that as a compliment because you come across as being very experienced and competent.

Ted Holmes: Thanks!

Myra Beckson: Well, it's true.

Ted Holmes: Oh, anyway. Please let me know if you need help with the Woolspin account—or anything else, for that matter.

Myra Beckson: Thanks, Ted. You bet. Hope I can return the offer someday.

Ted Holmes (in his head): *I wonder if she has a boyfriend.*

CUBICLE DRONE: We all hit the brakes when we see a police car on the side of the road. We pay extra attention when running a yellow light if we know it has a camera mounted to it. Surveillance cameras everywhere deter criminals from acting on their impulses and catch on film those who have no self-control. Convenience-store cameras provide video coverage featuring violent acts of unconscionable brutality rivaled only by Shark Week on the Discovery Channel. Cameras are nearly everywhere, and it's the first thing would-be criminals look for prior to committing a crime. We use video cameras to protect our houses, to document illegal activity, and to deter illicit behavior. Video cameras are powerful tools in fighting crime, and the threat of being videotaped is a powerful disincentive, not because it makes crooks better people by putting love in their hearts, but because it makes them better people by putting fear in their hearts.

Even the military uses drones, which are essentially flying video cameras with weapons attached, to hunt Al Qaeda and other terrorists. Up to this point the armed forces have been more or less chasing the terrorists, with respectable results. It's pretty much been a cat-and-mouse game with the future of freedom of speech, equal rights, bikinis and jeans, secular education, and personal liberty hanging in the balance. However, what they should try is baiting the terrorists. They should, for example, place a pile of books, preferably a mix of classics like *Don Quixote* or *Gulliver's Travels* and more modern novels such as *Portrait of the Artist as a Young Man* and *One Hundred Years of Solitude* or maybe, oh, a book about cubicle survival. Ahem. Also, for good measure, throw in *The Satanic Verses* by Salman Rushdie. Next, in that pile of books, they should also include an AC/DC CD—actually, the AC/DC CD *Back in Black*—several copies of *Maxim*, and a six-pack of Sierra Nevada. Then, when the terrorists come out of their holes and tunnels to burn the freedom pile with gasoline and lighters, the drone, with its eagle-eye camera can, as they say in the British SAS, "Give them the good news." Of course, when protecting your cubicle from far away, it's not necessary to take things this far.

Still, you can put that same drone fear into colleagues who wish to take advantage of your absence. Ever since the debut of computer video cameras, also known as webcams, people across the globe have offered live streams of their jobs, hometowns, favorite scenic views, personal affairs, and even twenty-four-hour real-time coverage of their existences. Webcams can be mounted on your monitor or an off-center location on your desk. Most are lightweight, unobtrusive, and provide high-quality audio and video. For Cubicle Drone purposes, however, you want a camera that sticks out, one that lets conspiring co-workers know that your cubicle is being filmed and that someone, somewhere, is watching. Place your camera in an ostentatious position atop your monitor; if it has some sort of light indicating that it's on, even better. Perhaps you could draw more attention to the surveillance camera by placing it on a colorful pedestal. Then, to make the camera more noticeable, leave an open operator's manual on your chair or beside your keyboard. It won't take long for those intending to pilfer your office chair, favorite stapler, ergonomic mouse pad, or beloved hole puncher to keep walking. Criminals are, if anything, lazy. They don't want trouble. They'll gladly move on to the next victim or wait for a better, easier opportunity to get something for nothing. Just to drive the point home, you may wish to leave a note on your chair or desk with the friendly message, "Smile for the camera!"

Quick Quiz Self-Assessment

(1) Which of the following sets of passwords is the best for Amanda Spinosa to use for her work log-in profile,

personal e-mail account, credit card information access, and bank account?

 (a) aspinosa1, aspinosa1, aspinosa1, aspinosa1

 (b) aspinosa1, aspinosa2, aspinosa3, aspinosa4

 (c) 19pota8toe1, 24ig26uana, i2dance4u, 6moo-shu15

 (d) spinosa1984, spinosa25, luv2dance, 615--wakeup

 (e) password, password, password, password

(2) Choose the most appropriate don't-mess-with-my-stuff tactic for Randy Joskow, whose kleptomaniac co-worker three cubicles down refuses to heed Randy's repeated requests to stop stealing his OfficeTime Pro-Level black pens with "autoprint" technology. They costs $4.95 for a package of six at StoreMart, and Randy is tired of having to make special trips and spending his own pocket money to replace them.

 (a) Lockdown

 (b) Three Mile Cubicle

 (c) Yellow Police Tape

 (d) Body Outline

 (e) Cubicle Drone

(3) True or False? The greatest benefit to being part of a corporate family is that everyone looks out for one another, and if for some reason a crime such as a theft does occur, the corporation will make every effort to catch the thief and make certain justice is served.

ANSWERS:

(1) Answer c. Password 19pota8toe1 because Amanda was born in 1981, in Idaho; 24ig26uana because she is twenty-five years old—between 24 and 26—and she has always wanted a pet iguana; i2dance4u because her dream is to be a professional dancer; and

6mooshu15 because every day she wakes up at 6:15 AM and her favorite Chinese food is moo shu pork. The others are too easily decipherable. It is important to mix numbers and letters. (2) Answer b, Three Mile Cubicle. Though the other techniques are effective, when battling a co-worker on a consistent, if not daily, basis it is best to make the threat immediate. The Three Mile Cubicle technique is perfect for this situation because perpetrators realize that if they enter and violate someone's personal cubicle space, there are imminent consequences. (3) False. Though corporations may make a sincere effort to curb and even solve crimes in the cubicle community, they are not, nor do they want to be, police officers. It is every individual's responsibility to take care of and protect personal property, even if it technically belongs to the company. Watch your back, especially when you are not around.

A Final Word

Cubicle employees must understand that being both successful and happy at work hinges on the ability to balance their professional lives and personal lives. Succumbing to the vast blandness of cubicle landscapes can transform even the most robust employee into one of those steer skulls people find half buried in the Arizona desert. However, rebelling against the cubicle landscape can turn even the most objective employee into one of those backwoods paramilitary types who fill the surrounding forest with hanging hubcaps and grade school rants about Jesus and freedom. In the corporate environment, becoming too acquiescent *or* too rebellious will lead to your demise. So be yourself but be professional; enjoy yourself but be cautious.

Cubicle life is like camping, but indoors. You're in a challenging habitat full of strange animals, and you need some things from home to help you survive and keep perspective. And despite their poor reputation, cubicles are more than likely not the reason unhappy people in your office are unhappy. Cubicles, after all, are just fabric, some steel, and wood.

Acknowledgments

I would like to thank my parents, Paul and Mary Thompson, and my siblings, Anne Marie, Trish, Paul, and Tim. Despite having been born on third base, I somehow ended up on first, but thanks to their support I am finding my way home. I would also like to thank my nieces and nephews for affirming that all of us are born innocent, except when playing board games. My cousins, especially the McManus family, have always had my back. Without Paul Caldwell, Scott and Wendy Taylor, Chris and Kiersten Camera, and Patrick Bardill, I would be alone on the floor of some bar somewhere.

Given that you can't take credit for choosing your family, I am most proud of my friends. Without Dave and Libby Cuttino, this book would never have been undertaken. Deep thanks go to my colleagues Brad McGuire, Bridget Morrison, Tony Laboy, Stephen Harkness, George Howell, Yi-Pe Hsieh, and Katrice Eborn for their kindness, professionalism, and humor. Molly Woods kept me sane throughout the writing process.

None of this would have happened without the talent and vision of my agent, Andrea Somberg at Harvey Klinger, Inc. Andrea is a writer's dream and an unassailable tribute to the often cryptic publishing industry. Special gratitude goes to editor Christina Duffy at Random House for being so encouraging, brilliant, and caring. Laura Jorstad is a consummate copyeditor and guardian of the English language. I haven't seen the written word covered in so much red since my dad gutted a cooler full of rockfish on the *Richmond Times-Dispatch*. Finally, I must thank Firefly Design Inc. for their tremendous illustrations and invaluable understanding of art, technology, and business.

ABOUT THE AUTHOR

James F. Thompson works in a cubicle at a television network in Washington, D.C. He has written for several national, regional, and online publications. He lives in Arlington, Virginia.

ABOUT THE TYPE

This book was set in Meridien, a classic roman typeface designed in 1957 by the Swiss-born Adrian Frutiger for the French typefoundry Deberny et Peignot. Frutiger also designed the famous and much-used typeface Univers.